Lean & Green
Cookbook for Beginners
2023

1500 Days of Fueling Hacks & Lean and Green Recipes to Lose
Weight Fast and Achieve Long-Term Results.
Easy and Affordable Recipes for a Healthy Lifestyle.
4 Meal Plans Included.

By DIANA POWER

Table of Contents

Introduction

Lean and Green is a low-calorie diet that mixes eating foods cooked at home with pre-packaged meals. This weight-loss plan combines prepared and homemade meals that are minimal in Calories, Carbohydrates, and fats to help you lose weight fast.

You have a lot of dinner choices if you follow the Lean and Green diet. Among them are branded goods and Fuelings or Lean and Green Meals for prepared meals.

In the following pages, you will discover every detail about lean and green diet, different meal options, and a wide range of recipes to choose from.

Fuelings contain all the nutrients your body needs to nourish itself properly while continuing to lose weight. However, you may run out of packaged Fueling and find yourself wondering how to replace them. In this book, you will find recipes to make your DIY balanced Fuelings: savory, healthy alternatives with Calories and nutrients to match your eating plan.

The secret of staying on the program and being successful is to be inspired every day about your weight loss program.

People often get into their lean and green meals, but soon they become so exhausted and can't wait for it to be over. This will not happen if you use this book to make the whole thing delicious, easy, and even funny! Thanks to this book, you'll have a variety of mouthwatering recipes for each meal, including a huge section of scrumptious Fueling Hacks.

Chapter 1: Lean and Green Diet Overview

1.1 What does it mean to have a lean and green meal?

Depending on your lean protein selections, a Lean and Green meal contains five to seven ounces of the lean protein cooked, 3 servings of non-starchy veggies, and up to 2 servings of the healthy fats. You can eat these Lean and Green meals whenever you like —

Whatever is most convenient for you.

1.2 Healthy Fats that are good for you

Include up to two servings of the healthy fats into the Lean and Green diet daily. Healthy fats are essential since they help your body function properly.

The body absorbs vitamins A, D, E, and K. They also aid in the normal functioning of your gallbladder.

1.3 The "Lean" Lean and Green Meal

Lean Suggestions:

• Portion sizes are calculated based on cooked weight.

• Choose grilled, roasted, broiled, or poached meats over fried meats.

• Eat at least two omega-3 fatty acid-rich fish meals each week (salmon, trout, tuna, mackerel, or herring).

• Meatless alternatives such as tofu and tempeh are accessible. As a vegetarian option.

From the list below, choose the proper serving size for any protein. Protein choices have been divided into three categories: lean, leaner, and leanest.

All of the alternatives are suitable for the Optimal Weight 5 and 1 Plan; this simply assists you in making educated meal choices.

Add two Healthy Fat servings to a 7 oz. Cooked meal.
Meatless alternatives:
14 whites of egg
2 cups of liquid egg white's replacement or liquid egg whites
Seitan (around 5 oz.)
1 1/2 cups (12 oz.) of cottage cheese (1% fat)
12 oz. of plain Greek yogurt, nonfat (0%) (15g carb every 12 oz.)
Cod, flounder, orange rough, grouper, wild catfish, haddock,
 tuna (canned or yellowfin steak), tilapia, mahi-mahi.
Crab, shrimp, scallops, & lobster are examples of shellfish.
Buffalo, elk, & deer meat
98 percent of the lean ground turkey or any other meat
Turkey (light meat).

LEANEST

Add 1 Healthy Fat serving to a 6 oz. Cooked meal.
Swordfish, trout, & halibut
Chicken: skinless breast or white flesh
95 percent-97 percent lean ground turkey or the other meat
Pork tenderloin or pork chops
Meatless alternatives:
4 egg whites plus 2 whole eggs
1 cup of liquid egg replacement plus 2 whole eggs
1 1/2 cups of cottage cheese (2 percent fat) (12 oz.)
12 oz. plain low-fat (2%) Greek yogurt (15g carb every 12 oz.)

LEANER

Choose a cooked amount of 5 oz. with no Healthy Fat serving.
Fish: salmon, farmed catfish, tuna steaks (Bluefin), herring, mackerel etc.
Steaks, roasts, & ground beef are all examples of lean beef.
Leg of lamb
85 percent - 94 percent lean ground turkey or any other meat
Dark flesh chicken or turkey
Meatless alternatives:
Mori-nu extremely firm or firm tofu (15 oz.) (bean curd)
3 eggs, whole (up to 2 times per week)
4 oz. Low-fat or part-skim cheese (1 cup shredded) (3-6 grams of fat per ounce).
5 oz. of tempeh
8 oz. of part-skim ricotta cheese (2-3g fat per oz.)

LEAN

Depending on your lean selections, add 0-2 Healthy Fat servings per day:
1 tablespoon of oil (any kind)
1 tablespoon of salad dressing (low-carbohydrate)
2 tablespoons of salad dressing (low-fat, low-carbohydrate)
5-10 olives (black or green)
1 avocado (12 oz.)
13 oz. of plain nuts (peanuts, almonds, pistachios, etc.)
1 tablespoon of plain seeds (sesame, pumpkin seeds, chia, flax, etc.)
½ tablespoon of margarine, butter, or mayonnaise (normal)

HEALTHY
FATS

1.4 The "Green" Lean and Green Meal

For each one of your Lean and Green meals, choose 3 servings from the Green Options list below. We divided vegetable choices into three categories: low, moderate, and high carbohydrate levels. Each one is acceptable on the 5 and 1 Plan; the list helps you make dietary choices based on knowledge.

Pick three servings from the Green Options menu:

½ cup veggies = 1 serving (unless otherwise specified)

Lower Carbs

1 cup: fresh or raw collards, endive, lettuce (iceberg, green leaf, butterhead, romaine), mustard greens, watercress, spinach (fresh or raw), spring mix, bok choy (raw).

½ cup: celery, cucumbers, turnip greens, white mushrooms, radishes, Swiss chard (raw), arugula, nopales, escarole, jalapeno (raw), bok choy (cooked).

Moderate Carbs

½ cup: cauliflower, asparagus, cabbage, eggplant, kale, a fennel bulb, portobello mushrooms, cooked spinach (scallop or zucchini), summer squash.

Higher Carbs

½ cup: chayote squash, broccoli, red cabbage, collard or mustard greens (cooked), green or wax beans, okra, kabocha squash, kohlrabi, leeks, (cooked) peppers (any color),
Tomatoes, turnips, summer squash (crookneck or straight neck), jicama, Squash, palm hearts, scallions (raw), and Swiss chard (cooked).

1.5 Condiments

To add extra taste to your meals, you may use condiments. It's just essential that you keep in mind that they contribute to your total carbohydrate intake. For best results, check nutrition labels for carbohydrate information and limit condiment amounts. A serving of condiments should include no more than 1 gram of carbs. You may eat up to 3 condiment portions per lean and green meal each day on all programs.

1.5.1 Fresh Herbs

Basil (whole leaves): 1 cup
Spearmint: 2 Tablespoons
Dill weed: 1 cup
Basil (chopped): ½ cup
Capers: 2 Tablespoons
Garlic (whole): 1 clove
Chives (chopped): ¼ cup
Parsley: ¼ cup

Cilantro: 1 cup
Rosemary: 2 Tablespoons
Garlic (minced): 1 teaspoon
Ginger root: 2 teaspoons
Lemongrass: 2 teaspoons
Sage: 2 Tablespoons
Peppermint: ¼ cup
Spearmint: 2 Tablespoons

.5.2 Dried Spices and Herbs

Allspice: ½ teaspoon
Bay leaf: 2 teaspoons
Anise seed: ½ teaspoon
Cardamom: ½ teaspoon
Basil (whole leaves): 2 teaspoons
Celery seed: 1 teaspoon
Basil (ground): 1 teaspoon
Cilantro: 1 Tablespoon
Caraway seed: ½ teaspoon
Cloves (ground): ½ teaspoon
Cayenne pepper: ½ tsp
Cumin seed (whole or ground): 1 teaspoon
Fenugreek seed: ¼ teaspoon
Chili powder: ½ teaspoon
Cinnamon: ½ teaspoon
Cloves (whole): 1 teaspoon
Dill seed: ½ teaspoon
Ginger (ground): ½ teaspoon
Crushed red pepper: ½ teaspoon
Coriander seed: 1 teaspoon
Fennel seed: ½ teaspoon
Curry powder: ½ teaspoon
Dill weed: 1 teaspoon
Garlic powder: ½ teaspoon

Mace: 1 teaspoon
Turmeric: ½ teaspoon
Marjoram: 2 teaspoons
Oregano (whole leaves): 1 teaspoon
Mustard seed (ground): 1 teaspoon
Nutmeg: ½ teaspoon
Poultry seasoning: 1 teaspoon
Onion powder: ½ teaspoon
Spearmint: 1 Tablespoon
Oregano (ground): ½ teaspoon
Pepper: ½ teaspoon
Paprika: ½ teaspoon
Parsley: 1 Tablespoon
Rosemary: 1 teaspoon
Poppy seed: 1 teaspoon
Salt: ¼ teaspoon
Pumpkin pie spice: ½ teaspoon
Tarragon (whole leaves): 1 Tablespoon
Saffron: 1 teaspoon
Sage: 2 teaspoons
Thyme (whole leaves or ground): 1 teaspoon
Savory: 1 teaspoon
Spice mixes: ½ teaspoon
Tarragon (ground): 1 teaspoon

1.5.3 Flavor Enhancers

Calorie-free sweetener: 1 packet
Liquid stevia: 5 drops
Crystal Light "On the Go" sticks: ½ packet
Monk Fruit In The Raw Sweetener: 1 packet

Mio: ½ teaspoon
Stevia In The Raw Sweetener: 1 packet
Truvia: 1 /3 packet
True Lemon or True Lime: 1 packet

1.5.4 Dairy, Milk Substitutes and Cheese

Butter Buds: ½ teaspoon
Cream cheese (light): 1 Tablespoon
Cheese – blue, feta, Parmesan (regular): 1 Tablespoon
Sour Cream (regular or light): 1 Tablespoon
Cheese – blue, feta, Parmesan (reduced-fat): 2 Tablespoons
Cream cheese (regular): ½ Tablespoon
Whipped Topping (Cool Whip): 1 Tablespoon
Cream substitute (liquid or powdered, regular): ½ teaspoon
Whipped Topping (pressurized): 2 Tablespoons
Cream substitute (liquid or powdered, sugar-free): 1 teaspoon
Greek yogurt (plain, low-fat or nonfat): 2 Tablespoons
The Laughing Cow Spreadable Cheese: 1 wedge
Kinds of milk:
Almond (refrigerated, unsweetened original or unsweetened vanilla): 1 cup
Rice (unsweetened): 1 Tablespoon
Cashew (refrigerated, unsweetened original or unsweetened vanilla): 1 cup
Cow's (unflavored): 1 Tablespoon
Coconut (refrigerated, unsweetened original or unsweetened vanilla): ½ cup
Coconut (canned, regular): 1 Tablespoon
Coconut (canned, light): 2 Tablespoons
Soy (unsweetened): 2 Tablespoons

1.5.5 Baking and Cooking Ingredients

Almond flour: 2 teaspoons
Imitation butter: 10 sprays
Baker's yeast: ½ teaspoon
Baking soda: 1 teaspoon
Baking powder: ½ teaspoon
Cocoa powder (unsweetened): 1 teaspoon
Bouillon: 1 cube
Broth or stock: 1/3 cup to 1 cup*
Cornmeal: ½ teaspoon
Cream of tartar: ½ teaspoon
Bran – wheat, rice, corn: ½ teaspoon
Extracts: 1 teaspoon
Coconut (shredded, unsweetened): 2 teaspoons
Lemon or lime juice: 2 teaspoons
Cooking oil spray: 10, ¼ second sprays
Lemon or lime zest: 1 Tablespoon

Wheat germ: ½ teaspoon
Liquid egg substitute: 3 Tablespoons
Onion (chopped): 1 Tablespoon
Nutritional yeast (small flakes): 1 teaspoon
Ranch dressing mix: ½ teaspoon
Nutritional yeast (large flakes): 2 teaspoons
Seaweed (fresh): 2 Tablespoons
Pine nuts: 1/8 ounce (~20 kernels)
Flax (whole or ground): 1 teaspoon
Seaweed (dried): 1 Tablespoon
Pumpkin: 1 teaspoon
Seeds: Chia: ½ teaspoon
Hemp: 1 teaspoon
Sunflower (kernel only): 1 teaspoon
Poppy: 1 teaspoon
Sesame: 1 teaspoon
Slivered almonds: 2 teaspoons

*depends on the brand and flavor – use serving size for around 1g carb or less

Barbecue sauce (regular): ½ teaspoon
Salsa (tomato): 1 Tablespoon
Barbecue sauce (sugar-free): 1 Tablespoon
Catsup (regular): ½ teaspoon
Honey mustard sauce: ½ teaspoon
Mustard (Dijon): 1 teaspoon
Catsup (reduced sugar): 1 Tablespoon
Cocktail sauce (regular): ½ teaspoon
Oyster sauce: 1 teaspoon
Fish sauce: 1 Tablespoon
Horseradish: 1 teaspoon
Mustard (yellow): 1 Tablespoon
Hot sauce: 2 Tablespoon

Soy sauce (regular or low sodium): 1 Tablespoon
Wasabi: ½ teaspoon
Sriracha: 1 teaspoon
Teriyaki sauce: 1 teaspoon
Steak sauce: 1 teaspoon
Vinegar (cider, white, wine): ¼ cup
Sweet and sour sauce: ½ teaspoon
Worcestershire sauce: ½ teaspoon
Syrups/flavorings (sugar-free Torani and Walden Farms, Inc): 2 Tablespoons
Tomato paste: 1 teaspoon
Vinegar (balsamic): 1 teaspoon

1.6 List of Healthy Fats

Saturated fats are commonly considered to be more harmful to your health than monounsaturated and polyunsaturated fats. The bulk of your healthy fat portions should come from those two groups. A portion of healthy fat should include approximately 5 grams of fat and fewer than 5 grams of carbs. The below healthy fats satisfy the requirements for one serving of healthy fat.

1.6.1 Monounsaturated Fats

Almond flour: 1 ½ Tablespoon
Guacamole: 2 Tablespoons
Avocado: 1 ½ oz
Kinds of milk:
Almond*
Olives: 5 to 10 black or green olives
Cashew*
Oils:
Avocado: 1 teaspoon
Peanut: 1 teaspoon
Canola: 1 teaspoon
Olive: 1 teaspoon

Nuts:
Almonds: 1/3 oz (˜8 pieces)
Peanuts: 1/3 oz (˜12 pieces)
Brazil nuts: 1/3 oz (˜2 pieces)
Hazelnuts: 1/3 oz (˜6 pieces)
Cashews: 1/3 oz (˜6 pieces)
Macadamia: 1/3 oz (˜3 pieces)
Pecans: 1/3 oz (˜5 halves)
Pesto: 1 Tablespoon
Pistachios: 1/3 oz (˜18 pieces)
Seeds:
Sesame Seeds: 1 Tablespoon

*unsweetened original, refrigerated or unsweetened vanilla: 2 cups

1.6.2 Polyunsaturated Fats

Margarine (regular): ½ Tablespoon
Mayonnaise (light): 1 ½ Tablespoon
Margarine (reduced-fat): 1 Tablespoon
Mayonnaise (reduced-fat with olive oil): 1 Tablespoon
Mayonnaise (regular): ½ Tablespoon
Nuts:
Walnuts: 1/3 oz (˜4 halves)
Pine: 1/3 oz (˜55 kernels)
Oil:
Flaxseed: 1 teaspoon
Sesame: 1 teaspoon

Grapeseed: 1 teaspoon
Soybean: 1 teaspoon
Safflower: 1 teaspoon
Seeds:
Sunflower (kernel only): 1 Tablespoon
Chia: 1 Tablespoon
Flax (ground): 2 Tablespoons
Hemp: 1 Tablespoon
Flax (whole): 1 Tablespoon
Pumpkin: 1 Tablespoon
Poppy: 1 Tablespoon

1.6.3 Saturated Fats

Butter: ½ Tablespoon
Cream (half and half): 3 Tablespoons
Coconut (shredded, unsweetened): 1 ½ Tablespoon
Cream cheese (low-fat): 2 Tablespoons
Cream cheese (regular): 1 Tablespoon
Kinds of milk:
Coconut (canned, regular): 2 Tablespoons
The Laughing Cow Spreadable Cheese Original Swiss: 1 wedge
Coconut (canned, light): ¼ cup
Sour cream: 2 Tablespoons
Coconut (unsweetened original, refrigerated, or unsweetened vanilla): 1 cup

Salad Dressings	1 Tablespoon		2 Tablespoons
Annie's Naturals	Goddess Organic Cowgirl Ranch Organic Smoky Tomato Organic Roasted Organic Goddess Garlic Vinaigrette Organic Green Goddess Organic Asian Sesame Organic French · Organic Caesar	Organic Balsamic Lemon and Chive Cowgirl Ranch Tuscany Italian Balsamic Vinaigrette Artichoke Parmesan Woodstock Vinaigrette	Lite Goddess Roasted Red Pepper

Salad Dressings	1 Tablespoon		2 Tablespoons
Hidden Valley	Avocado Ranch Simply Ranch Chili Lime Cucumber Ranch Roasted Garlic Ranch Sweet Chili Ranch Simply Ranch	Fiesta Salsa Ranch Simply Ranch Cracked Peppercorn Classic Ranch Ranch Cucumber Basil	Buttermilk Ranch Light Fiesta Salsa Ranch Light Cucumber Ranch Light Original Ranch Homestyle Light Greek Yogurt Cucumber Dill Greek Yogurt Spinach and Feta Greek Yogurt Lemon Garlic Greek Yogurt Ranch
Ken's	Balsamic Vinaigrette Three Cheese Italian Honey Mustard Creamy French	Greek Italian Red Wine Vinegar and Olive Oil Chef's Reserve Italian Chef's Reserve French	Balsamic Vinaigrette (Light Options)
Kraft	Buttermilk Ranch Cucumber Ranch Red Wine Vinaigrette Classic Ranch	Peppercorn Ranch Thousand Island Classic Caesar Roka Blue Cheese- Ranch with Bacon	Sun-Dried Tomato Caesar Vinaigrette Tuscan House Italian Zesty Lime Vinaigrette Zesty Italian Greek Vinaigrette
Newman's Own	Balsamic Vinaigrette Parmesan and Roasted Garlic Greek Vinaigrette Three Cheese Balsamic Vinaigrette Honey French		Lime Lite Vinaigrette Lite Italian Lite Caesar Lite Red Wine Vinegar and Olive Oil
Wishbone	House Italian Deluxe French Creamy Italian Thousand Island Spicy Caesar Sweet and Spicy French South of the Border Ranch Sweet and Spicy Honey Mustard Creamy Italian	Mediterranean Italian Light Blue Cheese Romano Basil Vinaigrette Bruschetta Italian Balsamic Vinaigrette Balsamic Italian Vinaigrette Light Parmesan Peppercorn Ranch	Olive Oil Vinaigrette Light Buffalo Ranch Greek Vinaigrette Light Thousand Island Light Creamy Caesar Light Ranch

Chapter 2: 5 &1 Meal Plan

This diet version is the most popular, with lean and green 5 Fuelings and 1 balanced Lean and Green meal per day.

Most people begin their weight-loss journey using the 5and1 Plan, an 800-1,000 calorie diet to help you lose 12 pounds (5.4 kg) in 12 weeks.

You'll consume 5 lean and green Fuelings and 1 Lean and Green meal each day on this regimen. Then drink one glass of water more each day than you do now. Whether it's in the morning with the Fueling or in the evening with your Fueling, it's a huge victory even if it's only one more glass in the evening. Keeping yourself hydrated is beneficial to your health and aids in the reduction of food cravings. Concentrate on consuming one more glass of water today and this week. On most days of the week, you should drink one meal every 2-3 hours and engage in 30 minutes of moderate activity.

The Fuelings and supper offer no more than 100 grams of Carbohydrates per day in total.

Lean and Green meals are rich in protein and low in Carbohydrates. 5-7 ounces (145-200 grams) cooked lean protein, 3 serve non-starchy veggies, and up to 2 meals healthy fats are included in one meal.

This Plan also contains one optional snack each day, which your coach must authorize. 3 celery sticks, ½ cup (60 grams) of sugar-free gelatin, or ½ ounce (14 grams) nuts are all plan-approved snacks.

Bear in mind that the 5and1 Plan strictly discourages the use of alcohol.

2.1 Meal Plan Example

Days	Fueling	Fueling	Fueling	Fueling	Fueling	Lean and Green Meal
1	Healthy Granola Bars	Green Smoothie	Chewy Cheesecake Swirl Brownies	Chocolate Flaxseed Energy Balls	Baked Parmesan Cheddar Crisps	Tofu Power Bowl
2	Egg Drop Soup	Flourless Protein Brownies	Avocado Strawberry Smoothie	Protein Pancakes	Super Energizing Chicken Soup	Tender Beef with Mushrooms
3	Protein Peanut Butter Balls	Chocolate Chip Pancake	Cheese Popcorns	Healthy Granola Bars	Granola Nut Cereal	Shrimp with Cauliflower Grits
4	Coffee Smoothie	Baked Parmesan Cheddar Crisps	Soft Cookie Dough Bites	Super Energizing Chicken Soup	Healthy Granola Bars	Vegan Meatballs with Zucchini Noodles
5	Protein Pancakes	Avocado Strawberry Smoothie	Chocolate Chip Pancake	Chia Raspberry Pudding	Soft Pretzels	Grill Salmon with Zucchini and Eggplant
6	Granola Nut Cereal	Cheese Popcorns	Super Energizing Chicken Soup	Protein Peanut Butter Balls	Chocolate Chip Pancake	Pan Seared Balsamic Chicken with Veggies
7	Caramel Smoothie	Chia Raspberry Pudding	Soft Pretzels	Flourless Protein Brownies	Avocado Strawberry Smoothie	Cinnamon Chipotle Pork Loin

Chapter 3: 4 & 2 & 1 Meal Plan

This plan contains 4 lean and green Fuelings, 2 Lean and Green meals, and 1 snack each day for individuals who require additional Calories or flexibility in their dietary choices.

If you want a flexible kind of meal idea to let you achieve a healthy and ideal weight, then 4 and 2 and1 Program is for you.

The 4 and 2 and 1 diet plan may help a diverse group of people. It is appropriate for you if:

- You'd want to include all food categories, such as dairy products, fruits, and starches.

- You have type 1 diabetes

- You suffer from type 2 diabetes

- You are 65 years old or older and are not physically active regularly

- You exercise for at least 45 minutes each day

- You need to shed less than 15 pounds

It's as easy as this:

- Consume four Fuelings plus two lean and green meals.

- 1 nutritious snack.

- Consume six meals each day, one every 2 to 3 hours.

3.1 Meal Plan Example

Days	Fueling 1	Fueling 2	Fueling 3	Fueling 4	Lean and Green Meal	Lean and Green Meal	Healthy Snacks
1	Protein Pancakes	Coffee Smoothie	Baked Parmesan Cheddar Crisps	Flourless Protein Brownies	Spaghetti Squash Lasagne Casserole	Baked COD with Feta and Tomatoes	3 Celery Stalks
2	Protein Peanut Butter Balls	Caramel Smoothie	Soft Cookie Dough Bites	Baked Parmesan Cheddar Crisps	Baked Cream of Cauliflower Soup	Quick and Easy Shrimp Risotto	10 Whole Almonds
3	Chia Raspberry Pudding	Avocado Strawberry Smoothie	Super Energizing Chicken Soup	Healthy Granola Bars	Lobster Rolls Low-Carb	Big Mac Salad	½ oz Pistachios
4	Flourless Protein Brownies	Green Smoothie	Granola Nut Cereal	Chewy Cheesecake Swirl Brownies	Toasted Ginger Sesame Chicken	Cauliflower and Alfredo Sauce	7 Walnut Halves
5	Chocolate Chip Pancake	Cheese Popcorns	Chia Raspberry Pudding	Avocado Strawberry Smoothie	Grilled Marinated Roast Garlic Flank Steak	Kabocha Pumpkin Pie	½ cup sugar-free Gelatin
6	Protein Pancakes	Soft Pretzels	Baked Parmesan Cheddar Crisps	Coffee Smoothie	Baked Tuscan Gateway Chicken	Spaghetti Squash with Feta, Basil and Tomatoes	10 Whole Almonds
7	Egg Drop Soup	Healthy Granola Bars	Super Energizing Chicken Soup	Caramel Smoothie	Pan-Seared Pork Loin	Veggie Egg Tofu Bowls	½ oz Pistachios

This plan is designed for maintenance and contains three lean and green Fuelings each day and three balanced Lean and Green meals.

Once you've reached your goal weight, you'll begin a 6-week transition phase in which you gradually increase your calorie intake to no more than 1,550 per day and introduce a broader range of foods, such as fruits, whole grains, and low-fat dairy.

After six weeks, you're supposed to switch to the 3 and3 Plan, including three lean and green meals and three Fuelings each day.

Like other Lean and Green Plans, this plan focuses on nutritionally balanced, small meals every two to three hours while including more food options in the appropriate amounts. Simply have three Fuelings and three balanced meals every day to complete the 3 and 3 Plan.

This plan offers a straightforward approach to maintaining a healthy weight by matching your food intake with your calorie expenditure. Remember that doing more exercise is an essential component of keeping a healthy weight.

4.1 Meal Plan Example

Days	Fueling	Fueling	Fueling	Lean and Green Meal	Lean and Green Meal	Lean and Green Meal
1	Flourless Protein Brownies	Coffee Smoothie	Protein Pancakes	Italian-Style Baked Tilapia	Shrimp with Cauliflower Grits	Low-Carb Sloppy Joes
2	Baked Parmesan Cheddar Crisps	Caramel Smoothie	Protein Peanut Butter Balls	Spinach and Cheddar Quiche	Low-Carb Taco Bowls	Basic Flank Steak
3	Healthy Granola Bars	Avocado Strawberry Smoothie	Chia Raspberry Pudding	Shrimp Vegetable Quiche	Bake Cheesy Chicken and Cauliflower	Cheese Burger Bombs
4	Chewy Cheesecake Swirl Brownies	Green Smoothie	Flourless Protein Brownies	Eggplant Kebabs with Charred Onion Salsa	Grilled Shrimp Zoodles with Lemon-Basil Dressing	Thai-Style Chicken with Zoodles in Peanut Sauce
5	Avocado Strawberry Smoothie	Cheese Popcorns	Chocolate Chip Pancake	Portobello Mushroom Pizza	Easy Surk and Turk Burgers	Pork Tenderloin with Mushrooms
6	Coffee Smoothie	Soft Pretzels	Protein Pancakes	Cajun Flavored Skillet Shrimp	Creamy Skillet Chicken with Asparagus	Cashew Chicken with Cauliflower Rice
7	Caramel Smoothie	Healthy Granola Bars	Egg Drop Soup	One-Pan Lemon Pepper Salmon with Asparagus	Super Easy Fish Tacos	Tasty Shrimp Fajitas

Chapter 5: 5 & 2 & 2 Plan

If you want a flexible kind of meal plan to help you achieve a healthy and ideal weight, the Optimal Weight 5 and 2 and 2 Plan is for you.

The Optimal Weight 5 and 2 and 2 Plan may help a diverse group of people. It is appropriate for you if you:

- You'd want to include all of the food categories, such as dairy, f Fruit, dairy, and Carbohydrates are all good sources of vitamins and minerals.

- You suffer from type 1 diabetes and are being carefully watched by your doctor.

- You suffer from type 2 diabetes and have to shed more than 100 pounds.

- Are 65 years old or older and are not physically active on a regular basis and need to shed more than 100 pounds

- Exercising for more than 45 minutes each day is recommended.

- You need to shed fewer than 15 pounds

- It's as easy as this:

- Include 5 Fuelings, 2 lean and green dinners, and 2 healthy snacks in your diet.

- Consume six meals each day, one every 2 to 3 hours.

5.1 Meal Plan Example

Days	Fueling	Fueling	Fueling	Fueling	Fueling	Lean and Green Meal	Lean and Green Meal
1	Baked Parmesan Cheddar Crisps	Flourless Protein Brownies	Protein Pancakes	Coffee Smoothie	Egg Drop Soup	Grilled Shrimp Marinated	One-Pan Shakshuka
2	Soft Cookie Dough Bites	Baked Parmesan Cheddar Crisps	Protein Peanut Butter Balls	Caramel Smoothie	Flourless Protein Brownies	Tofu Vegan Stroganoff with Mushrooms	Enchilada Bowls
3	Super Energizing Chicken Soup	Healthy Granola Bars	Chia Raspberry Pudding	Avocado Strawberry Smoothie	Protein Pancakes	Blackened Shrimp in Lettuce Wraps	Cilantro Lime Salmon
4	Granola Nut Cereal	Chewy Cheesecake Swirl Brownies	Flourless Protein Brownies	Green Smoothie	Baked Parmesan Cheddar Crisps	Cauliflower Bread Sticks	Pan-Seared Pork Loin
5	Chia Raspberry Pudding	Avocado Strawberry Smoothie	Chocolate Chip Pancake	Cheese Popcorns	Super Energizing Chicken Soup	Stir-Fry Asian Green Bean	Chicken with Garlic Cream
6	Baked Parmesan Cheddar Crisps	Coffee Smoothie	Protein Pancakes	Soft Pretzels	Healthy Granola Bars	Middle Eastern Style Meatballs with Dill Sauce	Tender Beef with Mushrooms
7	Super Energizing Chicken Soup	Caramel Smoothie	Egg Drop Soup	Healthy Granola Bars	Soft Pretzels	Lime Ginger Chicken and Noodles	Chicken Cheese Caprese

Days	1	2	3	4	5	6	7
Healthy Snacks	10 Whole Almonds	½ cup sugar-free Gelatin	½ oz Pistachios	7 Walnut Halves	3 Celery Stalks	½ cup sugar-free Gelatin	½ oz Pistachios
Healthy Snacks	7 Walnut Halves	3 Celery Stalks	10 Whole Almonds	½ cup sugar-free Gelatin	½ oz Pistachios	3 Celery Stalks	10 Whole Almonds

Chapter 6: Fuelings Overview –DIYs

Lean and Green "Fuelings," that include bars, cereal, shakes, cookies, and even savory choices like soup and mashed potatoes, make up at least ½ of any diet. Whey protein or soy protein are often included as the first component in these processed meals.

6.1 What are Fuelings, and what do they do?

Fuelings are the company's food items. There are three types of Fuelings: essential, classic, and select. To incorporate nutrition in your weight reduction journey, you may select from more than Sixty Fuelings in total. Essential Fuelings come in a variety of flavors:

- Decedent double chocolate brownie

- Vanilla cream

- Shake of the wild strawberry

- Bar with silky peanut butter and chocolate chips, and a lot more.

Fuelings includes 24 minerals and vitamins, high-quality, complete protein, probiotic, and no artificial colors, aromas, or sweeteners.

6.2 How to Use Fuelings?

The way you utilize lean and green Fuelings is determined by the program you're on. For example, the Optimal Health 3and3 Plan requires you to consume three meals and three Fuelings each day.

4 Fuelings, 2 green or lean meals, and one snack make up the Optimal Weight 4 and 2 and 1 Plan. The Optimal Weight 5 and 1 Plan promotes the idea of good eating habits. This diet consists of six little meals spread out throughout the day, five of which are Fuelings and one of which is a lean and green meal prepared at home.

6.3 How to Make Your Own Fuelings When You Run Out of Packaged Fuelings?

While purchasing packaged Fuelings is handy, preparing your own Fuelings at home is considerably healthier since you can avoid using unwholesome foods and chemical additives. It's also less expensive to prepare your own Fuelings. Simply ensure that you eat enough to avoid losing too much weight.

Choose fruits like pears, berries, apples, oats, peanut butter, cocoa, shakes, and bars. Nuts, seeds, roasted chickpeas, and whole-grain popcorn are some of the other healthy snack options.

It would be simple to replicate lean and green Fuelings with little effort at home if you run out of packaged Fuelings.

And here is a selection of Fuelings that you can prepare at home in a quick and easy way, with clean and healthy ingredients.

6.4 DIY Fueling Recipes

6.4.1 Healthy Granola Bars

Preparation time: 30 minutes

Servings: 10 (bars)

Nutrition facts per serving: calories: 114, carbohydrates: 21g, sugars: 12g, protein: 2,3g, fat: 2.7g

This recipe is vegetarian-friendly

Ingredients:

◊ 1 ½ tablespoon of almond butter

◊ 2 tablespoons of walnuts (chopped)

◊ 1 cup of rolled oats

◊ A pinch of allspice

◊ ½ cup of dates, diced and pitted

◊ ½ cup of orange juice

◊ A pinch of cinnamon

◊ ½ cup of dried cranberries

Instructions:

⇒ Preheat the oven to 375°F.

⇒ Spread the oats out on a baking sheet and toast for 10 minutes, or until they begin to brown.

⇒ After 5 minutes, toss the oats. Place the toasted oats in a medium-sized mixing dish.

⇒ Toss the grains with a pinch of cinnamon and allspice. Set them aside.

⇒ Blend or process the ingredients in a blender or food processor until smooth.

⇒ Mix the almond butter, dates, and orange juice in a small-sized saucepan. Heat the mixture on low for 15 minutes, stirring, until it is thick and sticky.

⇒ Mix vigorously until the oats are thoroughly covered with the substance in the dish containing the oats.

⇒ Combine the dried cranberries and walnuts.

⇒ Transfer to a shallow 8×8″ baking dish lined with parchment or plastic wrap and cover with a piece of plastic wrap. Form the mixture into a tight square using your hands.

⇒ Still covered, place them into the freezer to set for 15 minutes.

⇒ Take out and cut into 10 bars.

6.4.2 Flourless Protein Brownies

Preparation time: 25 minutes

Servings: 10

Nutrition facts per serving: calories: 111, carbohydrates: 9g, sugars: 5g, protein: 7,5g, fat: 6g

This recipe is vegetarian-friendly

Ingredients:

◊ ½ cup of pumpkin, diced

◊ 4 tablespoons of peanut butter

◊ 2 scoops of protein powder

◊ 4 tablespoons of cocoa powder

◊ ½ cup of chocolate chips of your choice

Instructions:

⇒ Preheat the oven to 350°F. Line a baking sheet with parchment paper on an 8x8 inch baking dish.

⇒ Mix the pumpkin, protein powder, cocoa powder, and almond butter in a blender, food processor, or large-sized mixing bowl and blend/mix until smooth.

⇒ Bake for 15 minutes, or until the mixture is cooked through, in a prepared baking pan.

⇒ Take them out of the oven, gently pushing the tops down using your hands to make them crinkly. Sprinkle with chocolate chips and let cool completely before slicing in 10 bars.

6.4.3 Egg Drop Soup

Preparation time: 20 minutes

Servings: 2

Nutrition facts per serving: calories: 122, carbohydrates: 8g, sugars: 3g, protein: 12g, fat: 6g

Ingredients:

◊ 2 teaspoons of coconut aminos

◊ ½ teaspoon of grated ginger

◊ 4 medium mushrooms, thinly sliced

◊ 2 large eggs

◊ 2 cups of chicken broth. low salt

◊ 2 green onions, thinly sliced

◊ ½ teaspoon of black pepper

Instructions:

→ Mix coconut aminos, chicken broth, mushrooms, ginger, onions, and black pepper in a medium-sized pot.

⇒ Bring to the boil, then reduce to low heat and cook until the mushrooms are soft, about 1-2 minutes.

⇒ In a small-sized cup, whisk together the eggs. To make egg ribbons, gently stir the egg into the soup as swirling. Serve warm.

6.4.4 Protein Berry Smoothie

Preparation time: 15 minutes

Servings: 2

Nutrition facts per serving: calories: 115, carbohydrates: 14g, sugars: 12g, protein: 13,5g, fat:1,6g

This recipe is vegetarian-friendly

Ingredients:

◊ 1 tablespoon of blueberries

◊ 1 tablespoon of honey

◊ 1 tablespoon of raspberries

◊ 1 tablespoon of strawberries

- ◊ 1 cup of almond milk
- ◊ 1 teaspoon of lemon juice
- ◊ 1 scoop of protein powder

Instructions:

- ⇒ Blend all of the ingredients until well smooth.
- ⇒ Place in the fridge for 10 minutes and serve.

6.4.5 Super Energizing Chicken Soup

Preparation time: 1 hour 10 minutes

Servings: 2

Nutrition Facts per Serving: Calories: 144, Carbohydrates: 18g, Sugars: 7g, Protein: 8g, Fat: 6g

Ingredients:

- ◊ ½ cup of shredded chicken
- ◊ A pinch of black pepper
- ◊ 1 cup of chicken broth
- ◊ 1 cup of water
- ◊ ½ celery stalk, diced
- ◊ 1 whole bay leaf
- ◊ ½ medium spaghetti squash
- ◊ 1 teaspoon of Italian seasoning
- ◊ A pinch of sea salt

Instructions:

- ⇒ Preheat the oven to 375°F.
- ⇒ Meanwhile, stir together all of the ingredients in a large-sized saucepan over high heat e, except for the spaghetti squash. Bring to the boil. Cover and reduce to a low flame. Cook for 30 minutes.
- ⇒ Prepare the squash by splitting it in half and removing all the seeds. Using a sharp knife, prick holes in the spaghetti squash.
- ⇒ Arrange bone half on a baking sheet and bake for 40 minutes (or until a fork easily penetrates the skin with just a little resistance).
- ⇒ When the spaghetti squash is cold enough to handle, scrape out the threads with a fork.
- ⇒ Remove the bay leaf just before serving and add spaghetti squash strands to the soup before serving
- ⇒ Serve hot or warm

6.4.6 Protein Peanut Butter Balls

Preparation time: 30 minutes

Servings: 4

Nutrition Facts per Serving: Calories: 128, Carbohydrates: 7g, Sugars: 2g, Protein: 8,6g, Fat: 10g

This recipe is vegetarian-friendly

Ingredients:

- ◊ 2 tablespoons of protein powder

- ◊ 1 teaspoon of vanilla extract
- ◊ 2 tablespoons of peanut butter, sugar-free, thick and creamy
- ◊ 2 tablespoons of peanuts, chopped
- ◊ 1 tablespoon of stevia

Instructions:

- ⇒ In a blender or food processor, mix the peanut butter, sweetener, protein powder, and vanilla.
- ⇒ Scrape down the edges as needed until the mixture is homogeneous. The combination should be thick yet pliable enough to push together. To taste, add additional protein powder if it's too thin.
- ⇒ To pick up dough balls, use a tiny cookie scoop (or a spoon). Roll into balls with cool hands if possible.
- ⇒ To coat the exterior of the protein balls, roll them with chopped peanuts.
- ⇒ To make the dough firmer and less sticky, place it in the freezer for approximately 15 minutes.
- ⇒ Keep refrigerated until ready to use.

6.4.7 Chia Raspberry Pudding

Preparation time: 10 minutes

Servings: 2

Nutrition Facts per Serving: Calories: 112, Carbohydrates: 9g, Sugars: 0,5g, Protein: 7g, Fat: 6g

This recipe is vegetarian-friendly

Ingredients:

- ◊ 1 tablespoon of protein powder
- ◊ 1 cup of unsweetened almond milk
- ◊ 2 tablespoons of chia seeds
- ◊ ½ tablespoon of stevia
- ◊ 3 tablespoons of raspberries
- ◊ 2 drops of vanilla extract

Instructions:

- ⇒ In a small dish, smash the raspberries.
- ⇒ Mix the protein, chia seeds, and powdered sweetener in a separate container.
- ⇒ Add the almond milk, vanilla, and mashed raspberries and stir to combine.
- ⇒ Refrigerate for at least 12 hours and serve with some raspberries to garnish.

6.4.8 Baked Parmesan Cheddar Crisps

Preparation time: 15 minutes

Servings: 2

Nutrition Facts per Serving: Calories: 115, Carbohydrates: 1g, Sugars: 0.1g, Protein: 8,5g, Fat: 8,5g

This recipe is vegetarian-friendly

Ingredients:

◊   4 tablespoons of reduced-fat cheddar cheese, shredded

◊   1 teaspoon of Italian seasoning

◊   6 tablespoons of Parmesan cheese, shredded

Instructions:

⇒   Preheat oven to 400°F. Using parchment paper, line a large-sized baking sheet.

⇒   In a small-sized mixing bowl, combine the cheeses.

⇒   Place consistent tablespoon-sized piles of shredded cheeses 2 in (5 cm) apart on the baking sheet. (Be careful to give adequate space since they will spread.)

⇒   Sprinkle with Italian seasoning.

⇒   Bake for 6-8 minutes, or until the sides begin to brown. (Keep an eye on them since they move from done to burnt quickly.)

⇒   Let the cheese chips cool completely in the pan before draining and crisping on paper towels.

6.4.9 Avocado Strawberry Smoothie

Preparation time: 5 minutes

Servings: 2

Nutrition Facts per Serving: Calories: 118, Carbohydrates: 32g, Sugars: 12g, Protein: 1,6g, Fat: 5,6g

This recipe is vegetarian-friendly

Ingredients:

◊   ½ avocado

◊   4 tablespoons of stevia

◊   1 cup of regular almond milk

◊   1 cup of strawberries (fresh or frozen)

Instructions:

⇒   In a food processor, puree all of the ingredients until smooth. As required, adjust the sweetness to taste.

6.4.10 Soft Cookie Dough Bites

Preparation time: 30 minutes

Servings: 4

Nutrition Facts per Serving: Calories: 123, Carbohydrates: 16g, Sugars: 2g, Protein: 3g, Fat: 5g

This recipe is vegetarian-friendly

Ingredients:

◊   1 tablespoon of softened butter

◊   3 tablespoons of unsweetened almond milk

◊   ¼ teaspoon of blackstrap molasses

◊   1 tablespoon of chocolate chips sugar-free

◊   2 drops of vanilla extract

◊   ½ cup of oat flour

◊   1 tablespoon of liquid stevia

◊   Pinch of sea salt

Instructions:

⇒   Using parchment paper, line a baking sheet.

⇒   In a large-sized mixing dish, combine milk, butter, and sweetener. To make the mixture fluffy, use a hand mixer.

⇒   Combine the vanilla and molasses in a mixing bowl.

⇒   Combine the oat flour and the sea salt in a smaller mixing bowl. In a large-sized mixing dish, mix the dry ingredients.

⇒   Using a hand mixer, mix until a crumbly dough forms. Taste and, if necessary, adjust the sweetness.

⇒   Combine the chocolate chips and fold them in. Make tiny balls using a small cookie scoop, approximately a tablespoon each, squeezing with your fingers as required. (It will be impossible for you to roll them within your hands.)

⇒   Place the cookies on a cookie sheet. Refrigerate for one hour before serving.

6.4.11 Coffee Smoothie

Preparation time: 10 minutes

Servings: 2

Nutrition Facts per Serving: Calories: 110, Carbohydrates: 9g, Sugars: 1,5g, Protein: 4,7g, Fat: 9g

This recipe is vegetarian-friendly

Ingredients:

◊   2 tablespoons of coconut milk

◊   1 tablespoon of peanut butter

◊   2 cups of strong brewed coffee

◊   ¼ cup of cocoa powder

◊   ¼ cup of sugar-free hazelnut coffee syrup

Instructions:

⇒   Fill an ice cube tray halfway with brewed coffee. Freeze until firm, at least 3 to 4 hours or overnight.

⇒   Blend the frozen coffee ice cubes, coffee syrup, peanut butter, coconut milk, and cocoa powder in a blender.

⇒   Blend until the mixture is smooth and creamy. If necessary, add more water to get the required consistency.

6.4.12 Chocolate Flaxseed Energy Balls

Preparation time: 15 minutes

Servings: 2

Nutrition Facts per Serving: Calories: 115, Carbohydrates: 7g, Sugars: 0,9g, Protein: 2,6g, Fat: 9g

This recipe is vegetarian-friendly

Ingredients:

◊   1 tablespoon of almond

◊   2 drops of vanilla extract

◊   1tablespoon of Golden flaxseed meal

- ◊ 1 tablespoon of peanut butter
- ◊ 3 tablespoons almond milk, unsweetened
- ◊ 3 tablespoons of unsweetened shredded coconut
- ◊ A pinch of sea salt
- ◊ 2 tablespoons of liquid stevia
- ◊ 2 tablespoons of sugar-free chocolate chips

Instructions:

⇒ In a food processor, blitz the almonds. Pulse until you have a combination of chopped almonds and almond meal (starting and stopping every few seconds).

⇒ Combine the flaxseed meal, shredded coconut, and salt. Pulse a few times, just until the consistency is consistent. (Be careful not to overmix.)

⇒ Combine almond milk, liquid stevia, peanut butter, and vanilla extract. Pulse once more until everything is blended. (Again, be careful not to overmix.)

⇒ Stir in the chocolate chips with a spatula and push them into the mixture.

⇒ Using parchment paper, line a baking sheet. Form the dough into 1-inch balls with your hands and put it on parchment paper using a tiny cookie scoop. You may eat it straight away, store it in the fridge, or freeze it.

6.4.13 Soft Pretzels

Preparation time: 25 minutes

Servings: 4

Nutrition Facts per Serving: Calories: 112, Carbohydrates: 4g, Sugars: 0,5g, Protein: 7,4g, Fat: 9g

This recipe is vegetarian-friendly

Ingredients:

- ◊ 1 ½ tablespoon of lukewarm water
- ◊ 7 tablespoons of blanched almond flour
- ◊ ½ cup of shredded low-fat mozzarella cheese
- ◊ 1 ½ teaspoon of active dry yeast
- ◊ ½ large beaten egg
- ◊ ½ teaspoon of stevia
- ◊ 1 teaspoon of baking powder

Instructions:

⇒ Combine the heated water and stevia in a medium-sized mixing dish. Set aside for 10 minutes after adding the yeast.

⇒ In a food processor, combine the almond flour, baking powder, and eggs. Add the yeast to the food processor after it has proofed and has risen in volume to around ½cup. Pulse until smooth.

⇒ Place the mozzarella in the food processor, with the cheeses positioned above the blade. Scrape the edges of the bowl using a spatula if required until a homogeneous dough develops.

⇒ Refrigerate the dough for 15-20 minutes, or until it is not too sticky to deal with.

⇒ Preheat oven to 400°F. Using parchment paper, line a large-sized baking sheet.

⇒ Shape a ball with the dough using greased hands. Cut it into 2 pieces, as if it were a pie. Make a long, thin log out of each piece, approximately 18 inches (46 cm) long. Twist one end of the pretzel into a pretzel by looping it around and down the bottom, then continue with the other end, passing over the first.

⇒ Place the baking sheet on top of it. Carry on with the additional dough portions in the same manner.

⇒ Season the pretzels with coarse sea salt and gently press them down.

⇒ Bake for 10-12 minutes, or until golden brown.

6.4.14 Cheese Popcorns

Preparation time: 25 minutes

Servings: 2

Nutrition Facts per Serving: Calories: 128, Carbohydrates: 1g, Sugars: 0.3g, Protein: 7,4g, Fat: 11g

This recipe is vegetarian-friendly

Ingredients:

- ◊ ½ tablespoon of coconut oil
- ◊ 1 teaspoon of white cheddar cheese powder
- ◊ 2 oz. of provolone cheese (make ½ -inch cubes)
- ◊ ¾ teaspoon sweet corn extract

Instructions:

⇒ Preheat oven to 300°F. Using parchment paper, line a baking sheet.

⇒ Place the 1/2-inch cheese slices on the parchment paper, spacing them out at least an inch.

⇒ Bake for 2-4 minutes, or until the cheese chunks melt somewhat and create rounded edges, but not too far.

⇒ Remove the baking sheet out from the oven. If the cheese spreads too much, use a tiny spatula or fingers to press the edges inside a little while it's still warm.

⇒ Let cool completely.

⇒ In a separate dish, mix the coconut oil with corn extract just before serving.

⇒ Toss the cheese popcorn with the oil mixture that has been seasoned with corn.

⇒ Mix in some white cheddar cheese powder, toss once more, and serve.

6.4.15 Granola Nut Cereal

Preparation time: 25 minutes

Servings: 6

Nutrition Facts per Serving: Calories: 113, Carbohydrates: 7g, Sugars: 0,6g, Protein: 3g, Fat: 10g

This recipe is vegetarian-friendly

Ingredients:

- ◊ 1 tablespoon of butter melted
- ◊ 4 tablespoons of almonds
- ◊ 3 tablespoons of pecans
- ◊ 1 tablespoon egg white

- ◊ 2 tablespoons of stevia
- ◊ 2 drops of vanilla extract
- ◊ 2 tablespoons of golden flaxseed meal
- ◊ 1 tablespoon of sunflower seeds
- ◊ 1 tablespoon of hazelnuts
- ◊ 1 tablespoon of pumpkin seeds

Instructions:

⇒ Preheat oven to 325°F.

⇒ In a food processor, pulse almonds with hazelnuts until most of the nuts are cut into big pieces (approximately ¼ to ½ of the entire size of the nuts).

⇒ Toss in the pecans. Pulse once more, stopping when the nuts are broken up into big chunks.

⇒ Combine the pumpkin, sunflower, stevia, and golden flaxseed meal. Pulse until everything is well combined. You want to save as many nut fragments as possible, and most seeds must be intact.

⇒ Fill the food processor halfway with egg whites. In a separate dish, mix the melted butter and vanilla extract, then evenly pour that in as well.

⇒ Pulse a few times, stir in a bit from the bottom to the top using a spatula, and pulse a few more times. Repeat as necessary until everything is uniformly covered. Avoid over-processing once again.

⇒ After this stage, you should have a coarse grain and nut bits mixture, with everything wet from the egg white and butter.

⇒ Place the nut mixture in a uniform layer on a prepared baking sheet and flatten it into a thin rectangle.

⇒ Bake for 15-18 minutes, or until gently browned on the edges.

⇒ Let it cool fully before slicing into pieces. (When you take the granola from the oven, it will be mushy, but it will crisp up as it dries.)

6.4.16 Chewy Cheesecake Swirl Brownies

Preparation time: 45 minutes

Servings: 6

Nutrition Facts per Serving: Calories: 114, Carbohydrates: 20g, Sugars: 3,7g, Protein: 4,7g, Fat: 7g

"This recipe is vegetarian-friendly"

Ingredients:

- ◊ 2 tablespoons of brewed coffee
- ◊ 2 tablespoons of almond flour
- ◊ ¼ teaspoon of baking soda
- ◊ ¼ cup of black beans, canned
- ◊ 4 tablespoons of stevia
- ◊ ½ teaspoon of double-acting baking powder
- ◊ ½ cup of fresh blueberries
- ◊ 2 to 3 drops of vanilla extract
- ◊ A pinch of salt
- ◊ 1 ½ tablespoon of natural unsweetened cocoa powder

- ◊ ½ teaspoon of liquid stevia extract
- ◊ 2 tablespoons of ground flaxseed
- ◊ For the Swirl:
- ◊ ½ teaspoon of liquid stevia extract
- ◊ 4 ounces of cream cheese (at room temperature)
- ◊ 2 drops of vanilla paste

Instructions:

⇒ Preheat the oven to 350°F and grease an 8x8" brownie pan.

⇒ Drain the black beans and strain them through a strainer. Clean well and drain any excess water.

⇒ Combine the black beans, vanilla extract, blueberries, coffee, and stevia extract in a blender. Purée until the mixture is smooth.

⇒ Whisk together the cocoa powder, stevia, almond flour, baking soda, flaxseed, baking powder, and salt in a large-sized mixing dish.

⇒ To make the cheesecake swirl, mix the stevia extract, cream cheese, and vanilla paste in a small-sized dish.

⇒ Pour the blender mixture into the dish with the dry ingredients and mix until everything is evenly distributed.

⇒ Fill the prepared pan halfway with the mixture and smooth it out evenly. Using a butter knife, swirl spoonsful of cheesecake swirl into the batter.

⇒ Preheat the oven to 350°F and bake for 40 minutes. Let cool fully before covering and storing in the refrigerator overnight. Using a sharp knife, cut the pie into squares.

⇒ Serve and enjoy.

6.4.17 Protein Pancakes

Preparation time: 15 minutes

Servings: 2

Nutrition Facts per Serving: Calories: 119, Carbohydrates: 27g, Sugars: 14g, Protein: 6g, Fat: 0,5g

"This recipe is vegetarian-friendly"

Ingredients:

- ◊ 2 egg whites
- ◊ ½ tablespoon of vanilla flavored protein powder
- ◊ 2 mashed bananas
- ◊ ¼ teaspoon of baking powder

Instructions:

⇒ In a mixing dish, whisk together all of the ingredients until smooth.

⇒ Heat a skillet over a medium flame, lightly sprayed with nonstick spray. Pour into the pan ¼ cup batter.

⇒ Cook for 4 minutes, or until the middle of the pancakes begins to boil. Cook for the next 2 to 3 minutes after carefully flipping.

⇒ Remove the pancake from the pan and continue the procedure until all of the batters have been utilized. In between pancakes, spray the skillet with nonstick spray as required.

⇒ Serve and enjoy.

6.4.18 Green Smoothie

Preparation time: 5 minutes

Servings: 2

Nutrition Facts per Serving: Calories: 112, Carbohydrates: 10g, Sugars: 6g, Protein: 3g, Fat: 7g

This recipe is vegetarian-friendly

Ingredients:

◊   1 cup of baby spinach

◊   ½ avocado chunks

◊   2 drops of liquid stevia

◊   ½ cup of almond milk, unsweetened

◊   1 tablespoon of hemp seeds

◊   ½ cup of strawberry slices frozen

Instructions:

⇒   In a blender, combine all of the ingredients and mix until smooth.

⇒   Drink immediately after dividing between two glasses.

6.4.19 Chocolate Pudding

Preparation time: 15 minutes

Servings: 2

Nutrition Facts per Serving: Calories: 113, Carbohydrates: 18g, Sugars: 0,6g, Protein: 4,5g, Fat: 9g

This recipe is vegetarian-friendly

Ingredients:

◊   2 tablespoons of cocoa powder unsweetened

◊   2 tablespoons of heavy whipping cream

◊   2 to 3 drops of vanilla extract

◊   2 tablespoons of granulated stevia

◊   ½ cup of almond milk unsweetened

◊   2 teaspoons of cornstarch

◊   1 egg

Instructions:

⇒   In a large-sized saucepan, sift together the sweetener, cornstarch, cocoa powder, and sea salt.

⇒   In a mixing bowl, whisk egg, heavy whipping cream, and almond milk gradually.

⇒   While whisking continuously, slowly stir the wet mixture into the dry mix, a little at a time.

⇒   Bring the mixture to a simmer over medium heat. Cook, whisking continuously until the mixture barely comes to a gentle boil. Remove them from the flame as soon as possible.

⇒   Let cool for 15-20 minutes before whisking in the vanilla essence.

⇒   Pour the mixture into four dessert plates. Refrigerate the dishes after covering them while they are still heated. Covering the puddings when they're still warm helps to prevent skin from developing on top.

⇒   Refrigerate for 4-5 hours and serve.

6.4.20 Chocolate Chip Pancake

Preparation time: 15 minutes

Servings: 2

Nutrition Facts per Serving: Calories: 112, Carbohydrates: 7g, Sugars: 1g, Protein: 6g, Fat: 9g

This recipe is vegetarian-friendly

Ingredients:

◊   1 tablespoon cream cheese

◊   1 teaspoon of baking powder

◊   1 teaspoon of stevia sweetener

◊   2 large eggs

◊   4 tablespoons of almond flour

◊   2 tablespoons water

◊   2 tablespoons of cocoa powder unsweetened

◊   ¼ teaspoon of vanilla extract

◊   2 tablespoons sugar-free chocolate chips

Instructions:

⇒   In a blender, combine all of the ingredients. To avoid getting caught at the bottom, start with an egg, water, then cream cheese.

⇒   Scrape down the sides of the blender as required to make it smooth. Let rest the batter for 2 minutes.

⇒   Preheat a nonstick skillet over a low flame. Pour about 4 tablespoons batter each pancake into the skillet.

⇒   When tiny bubbles appear on the surface, turn the pancake and continue to cook until both sides are golden. Continue until all of the pancake batters have been utilized.

⇒   Serve the pancakes hot or warm.

6.4.21 Caramel Smoothie

Preparation time: 10 minutes

Servings: 2

Nutrition Facts per Serving: Calories: 96, Carbohydrates: 14g, Sugars: 7g, Protein: 1g, Fat: 4g

This recipe is vegetarian-friendly

◊   **Ingredients:**

◊   1 ½ cups of almond milk (unsweetened)

◊   1 teaspoon of xanthan gum

◊   1 ½ tablespoon of sugar-free caramel syrup

◊   1 teaspoon sunflower oil

Instructions:

⇒   Blend all of the ingredients in a blender until the mixture is smooth and creamy.

⇒   If necessary, add water to get the required consistency.

⇒   Refrigerate for 10 minutes and serve.

7.1 Tender Beef with Mushrooms

Preparation time: 3 hours 10 minutes

Servings: 2

Nutrition Facts per Serving: Calories: 344, Carbohydrates: 10g, Sugars: 4g, Protein: 42g, Fat: 15,8g

Ingredients:

◊   1 ½ cups of low sodium beef broth

◊   12 ounces of stew beef, remove all visible fat, and cut into 1-inch chunks

◊   ½ tablespoon of garlic and spring onion seasoning

◊   1/2 cup of sliced button mushrooms

◊   Light cooking spray

◊   2 cups of sautéed zucchini noodles

◊   ½ tablespoon of Dash of desperation seasoning

◊   ¼ cup of sour cream

◊   ¼ cup of scallions

Instructions:

⇒   Heat a big nonstick frying pan on high flame with nonstick spray.

⇒   Sprinkle steak pieces with a dash of desperation seasoning while they're cooking.

⇒   Place the meat pieces in the skillet and brown them on both sides for 2-4 minutes.

⇒   Place the scallions and garlic and spring onion seasoning to the base of a large pot.

⇒   Place the browned beef on top of the seasonings and scallions in the pot.

⇒

⇒ ·   Return the pan to the flame, then pour in the broth, removing all brown pieces from the pan's bottom. Pour the liquid over the meat in the pot gently.

⇒   Cook the beef over low heat and cover for 2 hours.

⇒   Toss in the cut mushrooms. Cook for another hour or until the meat is fork-tender.

⇒   Mix in the sour cream until it is smooth and melted.

⇒   Serve immediately.

7.2 Creamy Chicken with Spinach and Tomato

Preparation time: 30 minutes

Servings: 2

Nutrition Facts per Serving: Calories: 351, Carbohydrates: 15g, Sugars: 1g, Protein: 43g, Fat: 13g

Ingredients:

◊   1 cup of artichoke hearts, drained and quartered

◊   ½ teaspoon of Dash of desperation seasoning

◊   ½ teaspoon of garlic and spring onion seasoning

◊   12 ounces of boneless and skinless chicken breast, thin slices

◊   ¼ cup of chicken broth low sodium

◊   Light cooking spray

◊   ½ can (15 oz.) of diced tomatoes (no sugar added) and drained

◊   ½ cup of baby spinach

◊   2 tablespoons of cream cheese, cut into small pieces

Instructions:

⇒   Heat a big nonstick frying pan on high flame with nonstick spray. Toss chicken breasts with a sprinkle of desperation seasoning while they're cooking.

⇒ Cook for 2 minutes per side, scorching the chicken in the pan.

⇒ Reduce to medium-high heat and stir in the tomatoes, broth, artichokes, and garlic and spring onion.

⇒ Cover and cook for 15 minutes over low heat.

⇒ Remove the lid, put the spinach, and replace the lid. Simmer for 3 more minutes.

⇒ Remove the cover, whisk in the cream cheese, and cook for another 2-3 minutes, or until the liquid has been reduced by half.

⇒ Serve hot or warm.

7.3 Mediterranean-Style Stuffed Pork Chops

Preparation time: 40 minutes

Servings: 2

Nutrition Facts per Serving: Calories:364, Carbohydrates: 2g, Sugars: 0g, Protein: 39g, Fat: 21g

Ingredients:

◊ 2 tablespoons of fresh rosemary, chopped

◊ 12 ounces of boneless pork loin (not tenderloin), cut into 4 thick slices

◊ Light cooking spray

◊ ½ teaspoon of Dash of desperation seasoning

◊ Butcher's twine

◊ 4 tablespoons of crumbled low-fat feta cheese

Instructions:

⇒ Using the outside burners, preheat the outdoor barbecue grill to 400°F. Do not cook the chops over an open flame. Alternatively, you may bake at 400°F for comparable results.

⇒ Make a pocket in the pork chops while they're cooking.

⇒ In a small dish, mix the rosemary with a Dash of Desperation.

⇒ Stuff 2 tablespoons crumbled of feta cheese into each pork chop and tie them with the butcher's twine.

⇒ Using nonstick frying spray, coat the top side of the chop. Toss an equal amount of rosemary mixture over each chop. To create the seasoning stick, lightly pat it with dry fingertips.

⇒ Place the chops in the middle of the grill (not directly over flames) and cook for 15 minutes on each side, or until a meat thermometer reads 150°F.

⇒ If using the oven, evenly arrange the chops in a baking dish and bake for 25-35 minutes, or until a meat thermometer reads 150°F.

⇒ Serve immediately.

7.4 Grilled Marinated Roast Garlic Flank Steak

Preparation time: 20 minutes

Servings: 2

Nutrition Facts per Serving: Calories: 277, Carbohydrates: 1g, Sugars: 0,3g, Protein: 30g, Fat: 15g

Ingredients:

◊ 1 teaspoon of garlic gusto seasoning

◊ 1 teaspoon of Dijon mustard

◊ 1 tablespoon of olive oil

◊ 10 ounces of flank steak

◊ ¼ cup of apple cider vinegar

◊ 1 teaspoon of Dash of desperation seasoning

Instructions:

⇒ In a big zipper-type bag, combine all the ingredients except for the steak.

⇒ Seal the bag and knead it to combine the marinade.

⇒ Place the steak in the bag and seal it tightly, pushing out as much air as possible.

⇒ Season in the fridge for 1 hour or up to all day.

⇒ Preheat the outside grill to 350°F and cook the steak for 3-4 minutes each side until the desired temperature is achieved.

⇒ For optimum results, slice against by the grain of the flesh on a diagonal.

⇒ Serve hot or cold over salads, sandwiches, and other dishes.

7.5 Big Mac Salad

Preparation time: 20 minutes

Servings: 2

Nutrition Facts per Serving: Calories: 383, Carbohydrates: 6g, Sugars: 2,5g, Protein: 32g, Fat: 25g

Ingredients:

◊ ¼ cup of tomatoes, chopped

◊ 1 tablespoon of onion, chopped

◊ ¼ cup of shredded cheddar cheese, low-fat

◊ ½ teaspoon of sesame seeds

◊ 2 cups of shredded lettuce

◊ 1 dill pickled spears, chopped

◊ 10 ounces of lean 95 - 97% ground beef, grilled

For the dressing:

◊ 1/8 teaspoon of onion powder

◊ 2 tablespoons of thousand island dressing

◊ A little sprinkle of stevia

◊ 1/8 teaspoon of white wine vinegar

Instructions:

⇒ In a small-sized dish, whisk together the dressing ingredients.

⇒ In a medium-sized mixing bowl, combine lettuce, pickles, tomatoes, ground meat, cheese, and onion.

⇒ Spread dressing with sesame seeds on top. Enjoy!

7.6 Low-Carb Eggroll Bowl

Preparation time: 25 minutes

Servings: 2

Nutrition Facts per Serving: Calories: 312, Carbohydrates: 7g, Sugars: 3g, Protein: 35g, Fat: 16g

Ingredients:

◊ 2 cups of cabbage, shredded

◊ 2 tablespoons of fresh green scallions for garnishing

◊ 1 teaspoon of Wok on seasoning

◊ 2 teaspoons of Valencia Orange Oil

◊ 2 teaspoons of sesame oil

◊ 2 tablespoons of low sodium soy sauce

◊ 12 ounces of 97% lean ground chicken or the turkey breast

Instructions:

⇒ In a small-sized bowl, combine the soy sauce and Wok On seasoning. Set them aside.

⇒ In a large-sized frying pan, heat the Valencia Orange Oil on a medium-high flame.

⇒ Cook, tossing periodically, for 8-10 minutes, or until the meat is browned.

⇒ Stir together the cabbage and also the soy sauce mixture in the pan. Cook for 3-5 minutes, or until the cabbage has wilted but remains crisp.

⇒ Remove from the flame and sprinkle with sesame oil before garnishing with scallion greens. Divide into two equal portions in bowls and serve warm.

7.7 Cheese Burger Bombs

Preparation time: 35 minutes

Servings: 2

Nutrition Facts per Serving: Calories: 320, Carbohydrates: 5g, Sugars: 3g, Protein: 33g, Fat: 17g

Ingredients:

◊ 10 ounces of 97% lean ground beef

◊ 2 zucchini cups, created from round zucchini by cutting in half and hollowing out, leave ½ of flesh into the bottom

◊ ¼ cup of low-fat shredded cheese of your choice

◊ 1 teaspoon of Quake steak seasoning

Instructions:

⇒ Combine the meat, Flavor Quake Steak Seasoning, and ½ of the cheese in a mixing dish.

⇒ Make two equal pieces and roll them into loose balls.

⇒ Fill each zucchini cup with one round of meat mixture. Cook for 15 minutes at 350°F in an air fryer.

⇒ Open your air fryer and add the remaining cheese to the burger bombs.

⇒ Cook for 1 more minute to melt the shredded cheese. Remove the burgers from the air fryer and serve.

7.8 Cinnamon Chipotle Pork Loin

Preparation time: 1 hours 15 minutes

Servings: 2

Nutrition Facts per Serving: Calories: 305, Carbohydrates: 1g, Sugars: 0,6g, Protein: 30g, Fat: 19g

Ingredients:

◊ 10 ounces of boneless pork loin (remove the visible fat)

◊ 1 tablespoon olive oil

◊ 1 cup vegetable broth

◊ 1 teaspoon of cinnamon chipotle seasoning

◊ 1 teaspoon of garlic and spring onion seasoning

Instructions:

⇒ Put the pork loin in a large saucepan

⇒ Sprinkle first with the Cinnamon Chipotle Seasoning, then the Garlic and Spring Onion.

⇒ Add vegetable broth and olive oil.

⇒ Cook over low heat for 1 hour until pork loin achieves a core temperature of 150 °F.

⇒ Remove the saucepan from the flame, slice, and serve.

7.9 Creamy Spinach and Garlic Stuffed Chicken

Preparation time: 50 minutes

Servings: 4

Nutrition Facts per Serving: Calories: 270, Carbohydrates: 3g, Sugars: 1,8g, Protein: 41g, Fat: 9g

Ingredients:

◊ 4 tablespoons of light cream cheese

◊ 2 cups of raw baby spinach

◊ 12 ounces of boneless and skinless chicken breast

◊ 1 pinch of Dash of desperation seasoning

◊ 1 tablespoon of garlic and spring onion seasoning

Instructions:

⇒ Preheat the oven to 375°F.

⇒ Place the chicken breast on a chopping board and cut a pocket into it with a sharp knife. Rep with the remaining chicken pieces.

⇒ In a large microwave-safe bowl, melt the cream cheese over high heat for 10 seconds or until soft and spreadable. If required, repeat in 5-second intervals. Season the cream cheese with the garlic spice. Toss to mix and smooth out any lumps.

⇒ Fill the bowl with spinach. Chop the spinach into smaller parts with a pair of kitchen shears.

⇒ Stir the spinach and cream cheese with a rubber spatula to get a uniform consistency. To avoid crushing and bruising the spinach, go slowly.

⇒ As many equal parts as you have of chicken pieces, divide the mixture. Fill the pockets of the chicken breast with the mixture. Rep with the remaining chicken pieces.

⇒ Place the chicken in an oven-safe dish, one on top of the other. Use a big enough dish to provide room between each item, so they don't touch. (This enables quicker and more consistent cooking.)

⇒ Remove the remaining cream cheese from the bowl with a rubber spatula and spread a thin layer on top of every of the chicken rolls to cover them during baking—season with a sprinkle of Dash of Desperation seasoning on each. If there doesn't appear to be enough cream cheese remaining, coat with a little nonstick frying spray.

⇒ Place the dish in the middle of the preheated oven, covered with aluminum foil.

⇒ Bake for 35 minutes, then remove the foil and bake for another 10 minutes, or until the internal temperature of the chicken reaches 165°F, as measured with a meat thermometer.

⇒ Let the chicken rest for 5 minutes before slicing and serving.

7.10 Pork Loin with Olives and Sun-Dried Tomatoes

Preparation time: 2 hours 5 minutes

Servings: 2

Nutrition Facts per Serving: Calories: 254, Carbohydrates: 2,6g, Sugars: 1g, Protein: 35g, Fat: 9,4g

Ingredients:

◊ ½ cup of chicken or vegetable broth

◊ ½ teaspoon of Mediterranean seasoning

◊ 12 ounces of pork tenderloin (without margination)

◊ 1 tablespoon of sun-dried tomatoes, thinly sliced

◊ 1 teaspoon of garlic and spring onion seasoning

◊ 10 green olives, sliced

Instructions:

⇒ Season the pork loin with salt and black pepper and place it on a large saucepan.

⇒ Pour the broth over the meat.

⇒ Sprinkle on the olives and sun-dried tomatoes.

⇒ Cover with a lid and cook over medium heat for 2 hours. If the meat is frozen, it may take longer to cook. When the interior temperature hits 155°F, it's done.

⇒ Thinly slice the meat, sprinkle with some broth, and top with a few olive and sun-dried tomato pieces.

⇒ Serve immediately.

7.11 Bake Cheesy Chicken and Cauliflower

Preparation time: 50 minutes

Servings: 2

Nutrition Facts per Serving: Calories: 404, Carbohydrates: 10g, Sugars: 4g, Protein: 48g, Fat: 18g

Ingredients:

◊ 1 teaspoon of roasted garlic oil

◊ 3 tablespoons half and half

◊ 3 cups of grated cauliflower

◊ 12 ounces of boneless and skinless chicken breasts, chunks

◊ 1 teaspoon of garlic and spring onion seasoning

◊ ½ cup of reduced-fat cheddar cheese, shredded

◊ Pinch of Dash of desperation seasoning

Instructions:

⇒ Preheat the oven to 325°F.

⇒ Heat the Roasted Garlic Oil in a large-sized pan over medium-high flame.

⇒ Add the chicken chunks, season with a sprinkle of Dash of Desperation, and cook until golden brown and tender (about 10-12 minutes.)

⇒ Meanwhile, chop the cauliflower into small chunks and shred it into "rice" in a large-sized mixing bowl. You may also do this in the food processor by processing a few pieces at a time.

⇒ Grease a 9x11 baking dish using nonstick cooking spray and arrange the cauliflower in the base of the plate in a single layer.

⇒ Sprinkle Garlic and Spring Onion Seasoning over the chicken in the pan. Stir in the half-and-half, trying to scrape all the browned pieces from the bottom of the pan.

⇒ Sprinkle the cheese over the cauliflower after pouring the chicken and cream mixture over it.

⇒ Bake for 15-20 minutes, until hot and melty, firmly covered with aluminum foil.

⇒ Serve hot or warm.

7.12 Basic Flank Steak

Preparation time: 20 minutes

Servings: 2

Nutrition Facts per Serving: Calories: 252, Carbohydrates: 2g, Sugar: 0.3g, Protein: 37g, Fat: 9g

Ingredients:

◊ 4 teaspoons of fresh lime juice plus an extra lime for garnishing

◊ 1/3 cup of low sodium beef broth

◊ 12 ounces of flank steak, remove all excess fat

◊ 1 teaspoon of garlic and spring onion

◊ 1 pinch of Dash Of Desperation seasoning

◊ 1 teaspoon of ground cumin

Instructions:

⇒ In a large zipper bag, combine all ingredients (excluding meat and Dash). Close the bag and mash all of the contents together with your hands to create a consistent marinade.

⇒ Add the beef, reseal the bag and place it on a platter. Refrigerate for about 1 hour or up to overnight.

⇒ Preheat the outdoor grill (or an indoor cast-iron skillet or grill pan) to medium-high heat when you're ready to start cooking. Before heating, gently oil the grates or coat the pan with nonstick cooking spray.

⇒ Remove the meat from the marinade and toss it out. Add a pinch of Desperation to the seasoning mix.

⇒ Cook the steak for 2 minutes on each side. Cook until the steak reaches an internal temperature of 115-120°F for medium-rare and 125-130°F for medium.

⇒ Remove from the pan and place it on a dish. Wrap it in a foil and let it rest for 10 minutes.

⇒ Serve the steak sliced on the diagonal, and garnish with lime wedges.

7.13 Chicken Scarpariello

Preparation time: 35 minutes

Servings: 2

Nutrition Facts per Serving: Calories: 258, Carbohydrates: 5g, Sugar: 2g, Protein: 36g, Fat: 9g

Ingredients:

◊ 6 ounces of boneless and skinless chicken breast

◊ ¼ sliced onion

◊ ¼ cup of low sodium chicken broth

◊ 6 ounces of turkey sausage

◊ 1 tablespoon of garlic and spring onion seasoning

◊ 1 cup of green peppers (bell, Italian, polao, etc.)

Instructions:

⇒ Using a 1/2" thick slicer, cut the sausage into 1/2-inch-thick slices (actually, kitchen shears work best for this)

⇒ Chop peppers and chicken into about equal-sized pieces.

⇒ Place a big frying pan with raised sides on the stove over medium-high flame.Add the sausage and cook, stirring periodically, for 2 minutes.

⇒ Add the chicken, peppers, and Garlic Seasoning to taste.

⇒ Cook, stirring regularly, for 18-20 minutes, uncovered.

⇒ Keep cooking for 1 minute, then remove from the flame and serve immediately.

7.14 Creamy Chicken and Asparagus Roulade

Preparation time: 50 minutes

Servings: 2

Nutrition Facts per Serving: Calories: 277, Carbohydrates: 5g, Sugar: 3g, Protein: 42g, Fat: 9g

Ingredients:

◊ 4 tablespoons of light cream cheese

◊ 1 cup of raw asparagus

◊ 12 ounces of boneless and skinless chicken breast

◊ 1 tablespoon of garlic and spring onion seasoning

◊ 1 pinch of Dash of desperation seasoning

Instructions:

⇒ Preheat the oven to 375°F.

⇒ Place the chicken breasts in a big zipper bag on a sturdy chopping board

⇒ Pound the meat with the back of a medium-sized, heavy frying pan while keeping the pan flat "slim. * Continue until all of the pieces are ½ inch thick.

⇒ Microwave the cream cheese in a microwave-safe bowl for 10 seconds on high or until soft and spreadable. If required, repeat in 5-second intervals. To smooth out any lumps, stir well.

⇒ Sprinkle Garlic and Spring Onion Seasoning over one-half of all the chicken pieces, then spread cream cheese equally over the other.

⇒ Arrange the asparagus on top of the chicken, allowing ½ inch between each piece. Each end is unrestricted.

⇒ Begin rolling the chicken into a "log" from one end and put the seam side down into a baking dish.

⇒ Rep until all of the chicken and asparagus have been used up.

⇒ Remove the remaining cream cheese from the bowl with a rubber spatula.

⇒ Spread a thin layer of cheese on top of the chicken rolls to cover them during baking—season with a Dash of Desperation seasoning sprinkle on each.

⇒ Place the dish in the middle of the preheated oven, covered with aluminum foil.

⇒ Bake for about 35 minutes, then remove the foil and bake for another 10 minutes.

⇒ Let the chicken rest for 5 minutes before slicing and serving.

7.15 Baked Tuscan Gateway Chicken

Preparation time: 45 minutes

Servings: 2

Nutrition Facts Per Serving: Calories: 328, Carbohydrates: 0g, Sugar: 0g, Protein: 40g, Fat: 18g

Ingredients:

◊ 12 ounces of boneless chicken thighs

◊ 1 tablespoon of Tuscan fantasy seasoning

◊ (or Garlic, Red pepper, oregano, black pepper, salt, thyme onion, parsley, and marjoram)

Instructions:

⇒ Preheat the oven to 375 °F.

⇒ Place the chicken in a baking dish that can accommodate all of the pieces without overlapping.

⇒ Season the meat evenly with the spice.

⇒ Bake the chicken for about 45 minutes or until it hits an internal temperature of 165°F.

⇒ Remove from flame and set them aside for about 5 minutes before serving

7.16 Tender Rosemary-Flavored Pork Loin

Preparation time: 30 minutes

Servings: 2

Nutrition Facts per Serving: Calories: 279, Carbohydrates: 3g, Sugar: 0g, Protein: 32g, Fat: 14g

Ingredients:

◊ 1 tablespoon of rosemary versatility seasoning (or Garlic, Rosemary, Parsley, Sage, Thyme, Salt Onion, Black Pepper)

◊ 12 ounces of pork loin thinly sliced, remove all excess fat trimmed

◊ 4 teaspoons of roasted garlic oil

Instructions:

⇒ Preheat the grill or the oven to 375 °F.

⇒ To create a paste, mix oil and seasoning in a small-sized bowl.

⇒ Dry the pork loin and season one side of each piece with equal quantities of spice.

⇒ Cook the pork chops onto the grill (or in a baking dish in the oven) until the internal temperature reaches 150°F. (If using the grill, cook for about 5-7 minutes on each side, or 20-25 minutes in the oven.)

⇒ Remove from flame and set it aside for 5 minutes, then serve.

7.17 Slow Cooked Finger Licking BBQ Chicken

Preparation time: 30 minutes

Servings: 2

Nutrition Facts per Serving: Calories: 223, Carbohydrates: 4g, Sugar: 3g, Protein: 33g, Fat: 7g

Ingredients:

◊ 1 tablespoon of Honey BBQ seasoning

◊ Pinch of smoked sea salt

◊ 12 ounces of boneless and skinless chicken thighs

◊ 1 tablespoon of southwest seasoning

Instructions:

⇒ In the bottom of your slow cooker, arrange chicken thighs in a single layer. (You may also use an Instant Pot, which takes 10 minutes to cook.)

⇒ Season the thighs with spices. Cover the slow cooker with the lid.

⇒ Cook for about 6 hours on low.

⇒ Remove the cover and shred the meat with two forks.

⇒ Serve warm over a salad or cold over a salad

7.18 Low-Carb Taco Bowls

Preparation time: 30 minutes

Servings: 2

Nutrition Facts Per Serving: Calories: 273, Carbohydrates: 4g, Sugar: 1g, Protein: 29g, Fat: 14g

Ingredients:

◊ 10 ounces of lean ground beef

◊ ½ cup of canned diced tomatoes

◊ 1 cup of cauliflower, steam it until soft

◊ approved condiments of your choice

◊ 1 capful of southwest seasoning

Instructions:

⇒ Preheat a big frying pan to medium heat. In a large nonstick skillet, cook ground beef for 8-12 minutes, or until slightly browned. With a spatula or a cutting instrument, break up the bigger bits into smaller pieces.

⇒ Season with salt and pepper. To mix, stir everything together.

⇒ Reduce the flame to low and cook for approximately 5 minutes, or until the liquid has been reduced by half, is lovely, and thick.

⇒ Choose a food processor or a chopping tool to chop cooked cauliflower into rice-sized pieces when the meat is cooking. If you're using ready-to-cook Cauli Rice, follow the package directions.

⇒ ¼ of the beef mixture should be placed on top of ½ cup cauliflower rice in a bowl.

⇒ Serve immediately with your favorite condiments.

7.19 Thai-Style Chicken with Zoodles in Peanut Sauce

Preparation time: 25 minutes

Servings: 2

Nutrition Facts Per Serving: Calories: 288, Carbohydrates: 6g, Sugar: 4g, Protein: 29g, Fat: 16g

Ingredients:

◊ ¼ cup of chicken or vegetable broth

◊ 12 ounces of chicken breast, thinly sliced

◊ 2 cups of zucchini noodles

◊ Light cooking spray

◊ 1 tablespoon of creamy peanut butter

◊ 1 teaspoon of Thai seasoning

Instructions:

⇒ Heat a nonstick pan over high flame, sprayed with nonstick spray.

⇒ Sprinkle Tasty Thai Seasoning over the chicken in a single layer. Cook for about 4 minutes, or until one side gets brown.

⇒ Turn the chicken pieces with tongs and cook for another minute or until done. Place the chicken in a dish and put it aside to keep warm.

⇒ Return the pan to the flame and pour in the broth. Remove all of the brown pieces off the sides and base of the pan using a spatula.

⇒ Add the peanut butter and stir it in until completely melted. Bring the mixture to a boil, then simmer until the sauce is thickened and reduced by half.

⇒ Toss in the zoodles and, using tongs, bring the sauce up through zucchini to cook. Cook for 1-2 minutes, or until zucchini is crisp and tender.

⇒ Return the chicken to the pan and toss it around with tongs until it is well heated.

⇒ Serve right away.

7.20 Easy Surk and Turk Burgers

Preparation time: 25 minutes

Servings: 2

Nutrition Facts Per Serving: Calories: 245, Carbohydrates: 1g, Sugar: 0g, Protein: 14g, Fat: 20g

Ingredients:

◊ 2 medium shrimps, peeled and deveined, and remove the tails

◊ 1 tablespoon of Scampi seasoning (or lemon, pepper, garlic, parsley, salt, onion, and celery)

◊ 8 ounces of ground turkey

Instructions:

⇒ Preheat the grill at 350 °F. (For stovetop directions, see below.)

⇒ Add the turkey to a large-sized mixing dish, season with salt and pepper, and toss thoroughly with your hands.

⇒ Form the turkey mixture into four patties.

⇒ In a heart shape, gently push two raw shrimp onto the top of the burger.

⇒ Cook for about 5-7 minutes on each side on the grill until done. The interior temperature of the turkey must be 165 °F.

⇒ Remove from the grill and serve with a delicious side dish

7.21 Charred Sirloin Topped with Creamy Horseradish Sauce

Preparation time: 20 minutes

Servings: 4

Nutrition Facts Per Serving: Calories: 373, Carbohydrates: 2g, Sugar: 0.4g, Protein: 35g, Fat: 23g

Ingredients:

◊ 2 tablespoons of low-fat sour cream

◊ 12 ounces of sirloin steaks, remove the visible fat, and trimmed

◊ 1 to 2 tablespoons of horseradish

◊ ½ tablespoon of salt, garlic, pepper, and onion powder mix

Instructions:

⇒ Heat the grill over medium-high heat.

⇒ Sprinkle Dash Of Desperation seasoning on both sides of the steak.

⇒ Cook on the grill for about 5-7 minutes on each side, based on how thick the steak is and how you want your meat cooked. If you want it rare, turn it down a notch. If you want it medium-well, turn it up a notch. Using the meat thermometer is the best method to cook the steak.

⇒ Make the sauce by mixing the sour cream with horseradish while the meat is simmering. To create a sauce, add one tablespoon of water at a time to thin the mixture. When you've finished, set it away.

⇒ After the meat is ready, just let it rest for 5 minutes on a cutting board before slicing thinly.

⇒ Serve with 1-2 tablespoons of sauce poured on top.

7.22 Low-Carb Sloppy Joes

Preparation time: 30 minutes

Servings: 2

Nutrition Facts per Serving: Calories: 335, Carbohydrates: 9g, Sugar: 4g, Protein: 36g, Fat: 17g

Ingredients:

◊ 1 cup of green bell pepper, diced

◊ ½ tablespoon of yellow mustard

◊ 12 ounces of lean ground beef

◊ ½ tablespoon of cinnamon chipotle seasoning

◊ 2 tablespoons of tomato paste

◊ ½ cup of low sodium beef broth

◊ 1 teaspoon of powdered stevia

◊ 1 tablespoon of garlic and spring onion seasoning

◊ 1 tablespoon of red wine vinegar

◊ Salt and pepper to taste

Instructions:

⇒ Sauté the ground beef in a skillet over medium flame on the stove. As the meat cooks, break up the bigger bits.

⇒ Simmer for 7 minutes before adding the other ingredients (excluding the broth) and stirring to incorporate.

⇒ After combining all the ingredients well, add the water and increase the heat to medium flame.

⇒ Set the flame to low, and then let the liquid simmer, uncovered, for approximately 10 to 15 minutes, until the liquid has been reduced and you have a beautiful sauce.

⇒ Enjoy while it's still hot!

7.23 Pan Seared Balsamic Chicken with Veggies

Preparation time: 45 minutes

Servings: 2

Nutrition Facts per Serving: Calories: 294, Carbohydrates: 13g, Sugar: 11g, Protein: 35g, Fat: 8g

Ingredients:

- 1 tablespoon of Tuscan seasoning
- ½ cup of cherry or grape tomatoes halved
- ¼ cup of water
- 12 ounces of boneless and skinless chicken thighs
- 1 tablespoon of Dijon mustard
- 1 cup of zucchini slices
- 2 tablespoons of balsamic reduction

Instructions:

- In a dish big enough to contain the chicken, whisk together the balsamic, mustard, and spice.Toss in the chicken to coat it. Refrigerate for at least 20 minutes and up to about 8 hours to marinate.
- Preheat the oven to 425 °F.
- Put a well-seasoned cast-iron pan over medium-high flame, big enough to accommodate all of the chicken without crowding.
- Place the chicken in the pan after shaking off the excess marinade (keeping it in the dish for later). Cook for about 10 minutes, or until charred and gently browned. Cook for another 10 minutes on the opposite side of the chicken.
- Prepare the veggies while the chicken is cooking.
- Using a whisk, mix the leftover marinade in the dish with the water.
- Arrange the veggies in a circle around the pan. Add a sprinkle of salt and pepper to taste.
- Pour the marinade over the vegetables and chicken. Toss everything together. Cook for another 15 minutes in the preheated oven.
- Remove from the oven and serve immediately.

7.24 Toasted Ginger Sesame Chicken

Preparation time: 25 minutes

Servings: 2

Nutrition Facts per Serving: Calories: 250, Carbohydrates: 1g, Sugar: 2g, Protein: 38g, Fat: 9g

Ingredients:

◊ 12 ounces of boneless and skinless chicken breast

◊ 2 teaspoons of olive oil and orange zest

◊ 1 tablespoon mixture of ground and toasted sesame seeds, onion powder, red pepper, salt, garlic, pepper, ground ginger and lemon

Instructions:

⇒ Place the chicken breasts on a chopping board.

⇒ Flatten your chicken breasts to about 3/8" thickness using a meat mallet or the backside of a frying pan.

⇒ Season with salt and black pepper.

⇒ In a large-sized nonstick frying pan, heat the Valencia Orange Oil over medium-high heat.

⇒ Cook for 7-8 minutes on one side, until a nice crust has formed—it should be somewhat golden.

⇒ Cook for a further 7-8 minutes on the opposite side and serve warm with a side dish of your choice or chilled over salad.

7.25 Creamy Skillet Chicken with Asparagus

Preparation time: 25 minutes

Servings: 2

Nutrition Facts per Serving: Calories: 337, Carbohydrates: 8g, Sugar: 3g, Protein: 43g, Fat: 14g

Ingredients:

◊ 1 tablespoon mixture of fresh garlic, chives and parsley, chopped

◊ 2 teaspoons of olive oil and fresh garlic

◊ 1 cup of fresh asparagus cut into 2-inch pieces

◊ 12 ounces of boneless and skinless chicken breast, make 1-inch chunks

◊ 4 tablespoons of light cream cheese

◊ Pinch of salt, pepper, and garlic powder

◊ ¼ cup of low sodium chicken broth

Instructions:

⇒ In a large-sized skillet, heat the oil over medium-high flame.

⇒ When the pan is heated, add the chicken breasts and cook, stirring regularly, for 7-10 minutes. The chicken must be gently browned before serving.

⇒ Add the broth into the pan and scrape all of the browned pieces off the bottom with a spatula.

⇒ Add asparagus and simmer for 10 minutes.

⇒ Combine the garlic spice, cream cheese and in a mixing dish. Increase the temperature to high.

⇒ Allow the cream cheese to dissolve evenly into the sauce by constantly stirring the ingredients. Bring to a boil, then reduce to a low flame and cook until a thick, rich sauce is created.

⇒ Serve immediately after dividing into 2 equal pieces and sprinkling with a salt, pepper, and garlic powder mix.

7.26 Middle Eastern Style Meatballs with Dill Sauce

Preparation time: 35 minutes

Servings: 2

Nutrition Facts per Serving: Calories: 261, Carbohydrates: 4g, Sugar: 1.4g, Protein: 30g, Fat: 14g

Ingredients:

◊ 10 ounces of lean ground beef

◊ Salt and pepper to taste

◊ 2 teaspoons of curry powder

◊ ¼ cup of low-fat plain Greek yogurt

◊ ¼ teaspoon of ground cinnamon

◊ a pinch of nutmeg mixture

◊ 1 teaspoon of fresh dill, chives, onion powder, and lemon mixture

Instructions:

⇒ Incorporate the seasonings with the beef and stir well to combine.

⇒ Make equal pieces of the mixture and roll them into balls.

⇒ Heat a nonstick pan over a medium-high flame and, once the pan is hot, toss in the meatballs.

⇒ Cook for 15-20 minutes, rotating the meatballs every 5 minutes to ensure even browning.

⇒ Prepare the sauce by mixing the yogurt and Dill spice while the meat is cooking. Stir thoroughly and store in the refrigerator until ready to eat.

⇒ When the meatballs are done, put them on a dish and serve immediately with sauce.

7.27 Chicken Cheese Caprese

Preparation time: 35 minutes

Servings: 2

Nutrition Facts per Serving: Calories: 298, Carbohydrates: 3g, Sugar: 1g, Protein: 42g, Fat: 12g

Ingredients:

◊ 12 ounces of boneless and skinless chicken breasts, pounded into 3/8-inch thickness

◊ ½ cup of tomatoes, chopped

◊ Fresh basil for garnishing

◊ 2 teaspoons of olive oil and fresh garlic

◊ 1 teaspoon Tuscan seasoning (or make by mixing black pepper, garlic powder, onion powder, parsley, red pepper)

◊ 4 tablespoons of shredded low-fat mozzarella cheese

Instructions:

⇒ Preheat the oven to 350 °F.

⇒ Put the chicken in a big plastic bag and squish it with the back of a small-sized frying pan for the simplest method. Make sure you're working on a cutting board or another safe surface. You don't want your countertops to break!

⇒ Pour the oil into a big, oven-safe pan (no plastic handles!) over medium-high heat.

⇒ Season each chicken breast with Tuscan seasoning and place it in the pan once the oil is heated.

⇒ Cook for 5-7 minutes on one side before flipping to the other. Cook for a further 5 minutes.

⇒ Turn off the stove. Place a quarter cup of tomatoes on top of each chicken breast.

⇒ Over each chicken breast, sprinkle 2 tablespoons of mozzarella and a pinch of Tuscan Seasoning.

⇒ Cook for 7-10 minutes, or until the chicken is completely cooked and the cheese is melted. Use a meat thermometer to check the temperature. The internal temperature of the chicken must be 165 °F.

⇒ Remove out from the oven and, if preferred, top some fresh basil or other herbs. Serve immediately with a side dish of your choice.

7.28 Pan Seared Beef Tips with Mushrooms

Preparation time: 35 minutes

Servings: 2

Nutrition Facts per Serving: Calories: 256, Carbohydrates: 4.8g, Sugar: 2g, Protein: 43g, Fat: 7.8g

Ingredients:

◊ 12 ounces of lean beef, make 1-inch chunks

◊ ½ cup of beef broth low-sodium

◊ 2 cups of mushrooms (small or whole)

◊ Light cooking spray

◊ 1 teaspoon garlic gusto (make your own by mixing parsley, garlic, and onion)

◊ ½ tablespoon mixture of salt, garlic, and pepper

Instructions:

⇒ Season the meat in a bowl with salt and pepper. Toss to coat evenly.

⇒ Set a well-seasoned cast-iron pan over a high flame on the stove. If you don't have one, a nonstick skillet sprayed with the nonstick spray will be fine.

⇒ Place the meat in a single layer in the pan. Simmer for 5-7 minutes, or until the meat has developed a rich, browned crust. To brown the other side of the meat, flip it over and continue the procedure.

⇒ Place the meat in a dish after removing it from the pan. To stay warm, wrap using a clean kitchen towel.

⇒ Increase the flame to high and add the broth. Scrape all of the browned pieces off the base of the pan using a wooden spoon. Stir in the Garlic Gusto spice and the mushrooms, and cook until the liquid has been reduced by half.

⇒ Return the meat to the pan and toss it in the sauce to coat it. Serve immediately.

7.29 Chicken with Garlic Cream

Preparation time: 30 minutes

Servings: 2

Nutrition Facts per Serving: Calories: 295, Carbohydrates: 2.8g, Sugar: 1g, Protein: 40g, Fat: 12g

Ingredients:

◊ Light cooking spray

◊ 1 teaspoon of fresh lemon juice

◊ 12 ounces of boneless and skinless chicken breasts, pound them into 3/8-inch thickness

◊ 1 tablespoon of butter

◊ 1 teaspoon of the natural sea and black pepper

◊ 2 tablespoons of low-fat cream cheese

◊ ½ cup of low sodium chicken broth

◊ Fresh basil, lemon wedges, or parsley for garnishing

◊ 1 tablespoon mixture of fresh garlic, salt, lemon, pepper, and chives)

Instructions:

⇒ Place the chicken breast in a big plastic bag and squish it with the back of a small-sized frying pan for the simplest method. Make sure you're working on a cutting board or another safe surface. You don't want your countertops to break!

⇒ Place the chicken in a large-sized nonstick pan over a medium-high flame and coat it with cooking spray.

⇒ Sprinkle a sprinkle of Dash of Desperation Seasoning on each chicken breast. Put the chicken in the pan once it is heated.Cook for 5-7 minutes on one side before flipping to the other. Cook for a further 5 minutes.

⇒ In a large-sized saucepan, combine the broth, lemon juice, garlic, and spring onions. To mix, stir everything together well. Scrape all of the delicious brown pieces off the bottom of the pan using a spatula.

⇒ Simmer for 10-12 minutes until the sauce has been reduced.

⇒ In a separate bowl, mix the cream cheese and butter.

⇒ Remove from the heat and, if wanted, garnish with fresh basil or other herbs, as well as fresh lemon wedges or slices. Serve immediately with a side dish of your choice.

7.30 Mediterranean-Style Roasted Chicken with Dill Lemon Radishes

Preparation time: 30 minutes

Servings: 2

Nutrition Facts per Serving: Calories: 240, Carbohydrates: 7g, Sugar: 2g, Protein: 18g, Fat: 4g

Ingredients:

◊ 1 teaspoon of salt, garlic powder, onion powder, black pepper and parsley

◊ 12 ounces of chicken thighs (remove skin)

◊ 1 tablespoon mixture of marjoram, garlic, rosemary, basil and onion

Instructions:

⇒ Preheat the oven (or the outdoor BBQ grill) at 375°F.

⇒ Using a sprinkle of Dash of Desperation Seasoning, season the chicken.

⇒ Place the chicken in a baking dish big enough to accommodate them all without touching.

⇒ Season the chicken with a pinch of Mediterranean spice.

⇒ Preheat oven at 350°F and bake for 30 minutes, or until chicken reaches 165°F.

⇒ Remove out from the oven and serve hot or cold over salad leaves.

7.31 Pork Tenderloin with Mushrooms

Preparation time: 30 minutes

Servings: 2

Nutrition Facts per Serving: Calories: 272, Carbohydrates: 11g, Sugar: 5g, Protein: 42g, Fat: 7g

Ingredients:

◊ 12 ounces of pork tenderloin

◊ ½ cup of chicken broth low-sodium

◊ Light cooking spray

◊ Fresh parsley for garnishing

◊ 1 teaspoon mixture of garlic, black pepper, onion, salt, and parsley)

◊ 2 cups of Portobello mushroom caps

◊ 1 tablespoon garlic gusto (make your own by mixing salt, garlic, pepper, paprika, onion, and parsley)

Instructions:

⇒ Preheat the oven (or an outside grill) to 400 °F.

⇒ With seasoning mix, coat on both sides of the tenderloin

⇒ Set a cast-iron skillet (or an oven-safe pan) on high heat on the stove. Using nonstick frying spray, coat the pan.

⇒ Put the tenderloins in the middle of the pan after it's nice and hot, but attempt not to let them contact.

⇒ Cook for 2-3 minutes on each side until browned.

⇒ Set the pork aside after removing it from the pan.

⇒ Add the chicken stock, garlic spice, and mushrooms to the pan while it is still hot.

⇒ Scrape the browned pieces off the bottom and sides of the pan with a wooden spoon. Only 1 minute of cooking time is required.

⇒ Return the pork tenderloin to the pan and bake for 15-25 minutes, or until the meat is thoroughly cooked. Use a meat thermometer to check the temperature. Pork should be slightly pink at 145°F and medium at 160° F.

⇒ Remove it from the oven when it reaches the correct temperature and set it aside for about 3 minutes before slicing. Note: If you cook pork for longer than the required time, it will become dry and overcooked.

⇒ Slice the pork and serve it with the sauce and mushrooms.

⇒

7.32 Pan-Seared Pork Loin

Preparation time: 30 minutes

Servings: 2

Nutrition Facts per Serving: Calories: 207, Carbohydrates: 0.4g, Sugar: 0.4g, Protein: 35g, Fat: 6g

Ingredients:

◊ 1 teaspoon mixture of black pepper, onion, salt, and parsley

◊ Light cooking spray

◊ 1 lb. of pork tenderloin

Instructions:

⇒ Preheat the oven (or an outside grill) at 400 °F.

⇒ Coat seasoning on both sides of the tenderloin

⇒ Set a cast-iron skillet (or an oven-safe pan) on the high flame on the stove. Using nonstick frying spray, coat the pan.

⇒ Arrange the tenderloins in the middle of the pan after it's nice and hot, but attempt not to let them contact.

⇒ Cook for 2-3 minutes on each side until browned.

⇒ Return the pork tenderloin to the pan and bake for 15-25 minutes, or until the meat is thoroughly cooked. Use a meat thermometer to check the temperature. Pork should be slightly pink at 145°F and medium at 160°F.

⇒ Remove it from the oven when it reaches the correct temperature and set it aside for about 3 minutes before slicing. Note: If you cook pork for longer than the required time, it will become dry and overcooked.

⇒ Slice the pork and serve immediately.

7.33 Lime Ginger Chicken and Noodles

Preparation time: 30 minutes

Servings: 2

Nutrition Facts per Serving: Calories: 349, Carbohydrates: 22g, Sugar: 3g, Protein: 42g, Fat: 9g

Ingredients:

◊ 12 ounces of boneless and skinless chicken breasts

◊ 2 teaspoons of olive oil

◊ Juice of 1 lime

◊ 1 tablespoon of Thai seasoning (make your own by combining lemongrass, garlic, ginger, lime red pepper, salt, onion, orange zest, and pepper)

◊ 1 cup of prepared zucchini noodles

Instructions:

⇒ In a big zipper-type plastic bag, combine the first three ingredients.

⇒ To create the marinade, massage the ingredients together in the plastic bag.

⇒ Place the chicken in the bag, press out the air, seal the bag, and chill for 4 hours or overnight.

⇒ Preheat the outside grill when you're ready to cook the chicken (or indoor grill pan or the frying pan).

⇒ Cook chicken for 12-15 minutes on each side over a medium-high flame or wholly done. Use a meat thermometer to check the temperature.

⇒ Prepare zucchini noodles with a spiralizer while the chicken is cooking.

⇒ Enjoy your chicken over zoodles.

7.34 Cashew Chicken with Cauliflower Rice

Preparation time: 35 minutes

Servings: 2

Nutrition Facts per Serving: Calories: 288, Carbohydrates: 8.6g, Sugar: 3g, Protein: 35g, Fat: 12.5g

Ingredients:

◊ ½ cup of green bell pepper, make thin strips

◊ 2 teaspoons of unrefined coconut oil

◊ 12 ounces of boneless and skinless chicken breast, make thin strips

◊ ½ cup of cauliflower rice

◊ 1 scallion, sliced into thin medallions

◊ 1 tablespoon mixture of chives, fresh garlic, pepper, onion. salt and parsley

◊ 2 tablespoons cashews, chopped

◊ ½ cup of red bell popper, make thin strips

◊ ¼ cup of low sodium chicken broth (if needed)

Instructions:

⇒ In a large-sized frying pan, heat the oil on a medium-high flame.

⇒ Add the scallion when the pan is heated and sauté for 1 minute, or until fragrant.

⇒ Cook for about 7 minutes, or until chicken is opaque.

⇒ Season all of the veggies with salt and pepper. Cover and simmer for 5 minutes, or until the vegetables are crisp-tender but not overcooked.

⇒ Prepare cauliflower rice while the chicken is cooking.

⇒ Take the chicken mixture off the flame. Divide cauliflower rice into 2 equal servings.

⇒ Arrange the chicken and veggies on top of the cauliflower rice and add crumbled cashews. Serve immediately and enjoy.

8.1 Baked COD with Feta and Tomatoes

Preparation time: 30 minutes

Servings: 2

Nutrition Facts per Serving: Calories: 319, Carbohydrates: 6g, Sugar: 3g, Protein: 38g, Fat: 16g

Ingredients:

◊ 1 cup of tomatoes, diced

◊ ¼ teaspoon of kosher salt

◊ 14 ounces of Cod fillet

◊ 1 stalk of scallions, chopped

◊ 1 tablespoon of fresh whole basil leaves

◊ 2 tablespoons of olive oil

◊ ½ cup small zucchini, diced

◊ 1 small garlic clove

◊ ½ teaspoon of black pepper, divided

◊ ¼ teaspoon of dried oregano

◊ 2 tablespoons crumbled low-fat feta cheese

Instructions:

⇒ Preheat the oven to 425 °F.

⇒ Cook the garlic and scallions in 1 tablespoon of olive oil in a saucepan until fragrant (3 minutes)

⇒ Add tomatoes and cook over medium heat, occasionally stirring, for 20 minutes.

⇒ Cut the zucchinis lengthwise onto a mandolin to create 1/8-inch thick slices while the tomatoes are cooking; put aside.

⇒ Place the fish on top of the diced zucchini in an oven-safe casserole dish. Drizzle 1 tablespoon of olive oil over the fish, then season with salt and ½ teaspoon of pepper.

⇒ Cooked tomatoes with feta cheese go on top of the fish.

⇒ Bake for 20 minutes, or until the cod reaches a temperature of 145°F on the inside.

⇒ Garnish with basil and serve.

8.2 Grilled Shrimp Zoodles with Lemon-Basil Dressing

Preparation time: 20 minutes

Servings: 2

Nutrition Facts per Serving: Calories: 198, Carbohydrates: 10g, Sugar: 4g, Protein: 19g, Fat: 9g

Ingredients:

◊ 1 cup of zucchini

◊ 10 ounces of raw shrimp

◊ 2 tablespoons of sliced almonds

◊ 1/4 teaspoon of black pepper

◊ ¼ teaspoon of crushed red pepper flakes

◊ 1/8 teaspoon of salt

◊ ½ cup of cherry tomatoes halved

◊ 1 medium shallot, chopped

◊ 1 tablespoon of lemon zest

◊ ½ cup of basil

◊ 1 small garlic clove

◊ 1 teaspoon of olive oil

Instructions:

⇒ In a blender, mix one tablespoon of sliced almonds, one garlic clove, one shallot, red wine vinegar, red pepper flakes, ½ cup of olive oil, and lemon zest to make the lemon basil dressing. Pulse until smooth and evenly mixed—season to taste with salt and black pepper and put aside.

⇒ To toast the remaining tablespoon of almonds, place them in a small pan over a medium-high flame. Shake the pan every few seconds until the almonds are lightly browned. Take the almonds off the flame and put them aside.

⇒ Heat one tablespoon of oil over a medium-high flame. Season the shrimp with salt and black pepper. Cook shrimp for 6 to 8 minutes, then mix with two spoonsful lemon basil dressing. Set aside the seasoned shrimp in a separate clean dish.

⇒ Cut zucchini into thin spaghetti-like strands using a mandolin or vegetable spiralizer. Sprinkle the zucchini noodles with salt and pepper, then mix with an extra two spoonsful of the lemon basil dressing in the same skillet where the shrimp was cooked. Cook for 3 minutes over a medium flame until just soft. Turn off the flame.

⇒ Whisk the seasoned shrimp, zucchini noodles, and cherry tomatoes.

⇒ Sprinkle with toasted sliced almonds and serve.

8.3 Cilantro Lime Salmon

Preparation time: 45 minutes

Servings: 2

Nutrition Facts per Serving: Calories: 309, Carbohydrates: 9g, Sugar: 2g, Protein: 30g, Fat: 17g

Ingredients:

◊ 2 tablespoons of fresh lime juice (optional)*

◊ ½ teaspoon of salt, divided

◊ 1 cup of yellow bell pepper, sliced

◊ ½ teaspoon of black pepper

◊ 1 cup of fresh cilantro, divided

◊ 10 ounces raw salmon filets

◊ ½ cup of green bell peppers sliced

◊ 2 tablespoons of fresh lemon juice (optional)*

◊ 2 tablespoons of hot red pepper sauce

◊ 1 teaspoon of cumin

◊ ½ cup of water

◊ ½ cup of red bell peppers sliced

Instructions:

⇒ Put water, 1/2 of the cilantro, hot red pepper sauce, cumin, lemon, or lime juice, salt in a food processor, and puree until smooth. Fill a large resealable plastic bag halfway with the marinade.

⇒ In a separate dish, combine the salmon with the marinade. Turn to coat salmon after sealing the bag and squeezing out the air. Refrigerate for about 1 hour, flipping the bag now and then.

⇒ Once the meat has marinated, preheat the oven to 400°F. In a lightly oiled, medium-sized square baking dish, spread all pepper slices in a single layer and season with pepper and the remaining salt.

⇒ Bake for 20 minutes, rotating the pepper slices halfway through.

⇒ Drain the salmon and toss out the marinade. Using the remaining chopped, fresh cilantro, crust the tops of the fish.

⇒ Place the fish on top of the peppers and bake for 12 to 14 minutes.

⇒ Serve immediately.

8.4 Grill Salmon with Zucchini and Eggplant

Preparation time: 25 minutes

Servings: 2

Nutrition Facts per Serving: Calories: 338, Carbohydrates: 5g, Sugar: 3g, Protein: 35g, Fat: 20g

Ingredients:

◊ 1 teaspoon of McCormick Grill Mates fiery 5 pepper seasoning

◊ 2 slices eggplant

◊ 12 ounces of raw salmon filets

◊ ½ teaspoon of black pepper (optional)*

◊ Light cooking spray

◊ ½ cup zucchini sliced

Instructions:

⇒ Preheat your outside grill to High

⇒ Coat the tin foil using cooking spray. Apply one teaspoon of McCormick Grill Mates Fiery Seasoning (half on each side) on the fillet.

⇒ Place the salmon on a piece of tin foil large enough to wrap all around the fillet, skin side down. Bring the long sides of the foil together up and around the fish. To form a seal and prevent the fold from falling apart, fold the foil sides together.

⇒ Arrange the zucchini and eggplant slices in the grill basket—season with a pinch of black pepper.

⇒ Close the grill cover, place the salmon, and grill basket with veggies on the grill.

⇒ After 15 minutes, check the salmon for doneness; it will be done when it is light pink and fairly robust to the touch if pushed. After 15 minutes, flip the veggies in the grill basket. Cook for another 10 minutes. Serve immediately.

8.5 Shrimp with Spiralized Zoodles

Preparation time: 15 minutes

Servings: 2

Nutrition Facts per Serving: Calories: 152, Carbohydrates: 5g, Sugar: 4g, Protein: 18g, Fat: 7g

Ingredients:

◊   1 cup of zucchini spiraled

◊   ¼ teaspoon of garlic salt

◊   2 teaspoons of olive oil

◊   1 tablespoon of grated Parmesan

◊   1 cup of yellow squash spiraled

◊   8 ounces of cooked shrimp

◊   1 tablespoon of Rao's marinara sauce

◊   ½ teaspoon of Italian seasoning

Instructions:

⇒   Heat the olive oil in a medium-sized skillet over a medium-high flame.

⇒   Cook spiralized zucchini and yellow squash for 5 minutes.

⇒   Combine the shrimp, marinara sauce, garlic salt, and Italian seasoning in a mixing dish.

⇒   Add to the veggies and cook for about 3 minutes.

⇒   Place on a platter, top with Parmesan cheese and serve.

8.6 Italian-Style Shrimp and Broccoli

Preparation time: 20 minutes

Servings: 2

Nutrition Facts per Serving: Calories: 178, Carbohydrates: 5g, Sugar: 2g, Protein: 21g, Fat: 8g

Ingredients:

◊   1 cup of broccoli, chopped

◊   1 tablespoon of olive oil

◊   2 tablespoons of Ken's Lite Northern Italian with basil and Romano (optional)*

◊   2 tablespoons of Newman's Own Parmesan and garlic dressing (optional)*

◊   10 ounces of cooked shrimp

◊   ½ cup of cherry tomatoes, chopped

◊   ½ teaspoon of black pepper steamed

Instructions:

⇒   Use frozen or fresh shrimp (thaw as per package instructions).

⇒   Use frozen or fresh shrimp (thaw as per package instructions).

⇒   Heat 1 teaspoon of olive oil in a large-sized pan and put the broccoli and chopped cherry tomatoes; cook

for 2-3 minutes, or until veggies are tender-crisp. Remove the pan from the flame, cover it, and put it aside.

⇒   Toss salad dressing with shrimp and black pepper in a large skillet. Cook over medium heat until the shrimp is done (opaque in color).

⇒   Add the veggies to the shrimp skillet and cook for 2-3 minutes to warm the veggies.

⇒   Place the shrimp and veggies on a dish and mix the Parmesan cheese.

⇒   Serve immediately.

8.7 Garlic Flavored Shrimp with Zucchini Noodles

Preparation time: 20 minutes

Servings: 2

Nutrition Facts per Serving: Calories: 175, Carbohydrates: 5g, Sugar: 2g, Protein: 17g, Fat: 8g

Ingredients:

◊   2 teaspoons of olive oil

◊   1 teaspoon of fresh lemon juice

◊   ½ cup of grape tomatoes halved

◊   10 ounces of raw shrimp

◊   1 teaspoon of fresh parsley, minced

◊   ½ tablespoon of light butter

◊   1 tablespoon of Parmesan cheese

◊   1 teaspoon of garlic, minced

◊   1/8 teaspoon of crushed red pepper

◊   1 cup of zucchini noodles

Instructions:

⇒   Heat one teaspoon of olive oil in a big pan on a medium-high flame, add the shrimp and cook for 4-5 minutes.

⇒   Toss the butter, garlic, lemon juice, parsley, red pepper flakes, and tomatoes into the pan once the shrimp has become pink.

⇒   Add one teaspoon of olive oil in a separate skillet sauté the zucchini noodles for about 4 minutes over a medium-high flame. Put the zucchini noodles in at the last minute to avoid overcooking them.

⇒   Place the zucchini noodles on a plate, add the shrimp mixture, then top with one tablespoon of Parmesan cheese and serve.

8.8 Tasty Shrimp Fajitas

Preparation time: 40 minutes

Servings: 2

Nutrition Facts per Serving: Calories: 306, Carbohydrates: 15g, Sugar: 4g, Protein: 24g, Fat: 17g

Ingredients:

◊   2 teaspoons of Cajun seasoning

◊   ½ cup of zucchini grated

◊   8 ounces of raw shrimp

- ◊ ¼ cup of eggs
- ◊ 2 teaspoons of olive oil
- ◊ 1/8 teaspoon of Mrs. Dash southwest chipotle
- ◊ 1 cup of red peppers sliced
- ◊ 3/8 cup of low-fat Mexican cheese blend
- ◊ 1 cup of yellow bell pepper sliced
- ◊ ¼ cup of frozen riced cauliflower
- ◊ ½ medium avocado sliced

Instructions:

⇒ Preheat the oven to 400 °F.

⇒ Heat 2 teaspoons of olive oil on the medium-high flame in a large-sized skillet. Cook for about 4-5 minutes, or until shrimp is pink, adding peppers, shrimp, and Cajun spice.

⇒ Recipe for Mini Tortilla Shells: Microwave the cauliflower rice for 2 minutes, cool, and press out the excess water in a (tea towel or cheesecloth).

⇒ Do not microwave the zucchini; instead, sprinkle with 1/8 teaspoon Mrs. Dash and set aside 15 minutes before squeezing out any extra water.

⇒ Combine the egg beaters, cheese, and cauliflower, and zucchini to form four tiny circles.

⇒ Spray a cookie sheet covered with parchment paper with nonstick cooking spray. Bake for 15 minutes, then turn halfway through and cook for another 15 minutes.

⇒ Fill small tortillas halfway with shrimp and peppers, then top with avocado slices and serve.

8.9 One-Pan Lemon Pepper Salmon with Asparagus

Preparation time: 25 minutes

Servings: 2

Nutrition Facts per Serving: Calories: 391, Carbohydrates: 7g, Sugar: 3g, Protein: 41g, Fat: 22g

Ingredients:

- ◊ Light cooking spray
- ◊ 1/8 teaspoon of salt (optional)*
- ◊ 2 cups of asparagus
- ◊ ¼ cup of grated Parmesan cheese
- ◊ 12 ounces of salmon
- ◊ 2 teaspoons of lemon pepper seasoning - salt-free
- ◊ ½ teaspoon of garlic powder

- • 1 medium lemon sliced

Instructions:

⇒ Preheat the oven to 400°F.

⇒ Place the salmon in the middle of a foil-lined, lightly oiled baking sheet.

⇒ Season the salmon with lemon pepper spice and salt, if preferred, and top with lemon slices.

⇒ Mix Parmesan cheese and garlic powder in a small-sized bowl.

⇒ Spray the asparagus spears gently with cooking spray and arrange them over the fish.

⇒ Toss the asparagus with a combination of Parmesan cheese and garlic powder.

⇒ Bake for 15 to 20 minutes and serve immediately.

8.10 Sheet-Pan Shrimp Scampi

Preparation time: 15 minutes

Servings: 2

Nutrition Facts per Serving: Calories: 208, Carbohydrates: 5g, Sugar: 2g, Protein: 21g, Fat: 10g

Ingredients:

- ◊ 12 ounces of shrimp, finely chopped
- ◊ 1 teaspoon of olive oil
- ◊ 1 small lemon juice
- ◊ ¼ teaspoon of salt (optional)*
- ◊ 1 cup small, zucchini
- ◊ 2 tablespoons of Parmesan cheese grated
- ◊ 1 tablespoon of unsalted butter melted
- ◊ 1 small garlic clove, minced

Instructions:

⇒ Preheat the oven to 400 °F.

⇒ Chop the zucchini into fine ribbons using a vegetable peeler.

⇒ Combine zucchini ribbons and other ingredients in a large-sized resealable plastic bag. Seal the bag and toss the zucchini and shrimp in it to evenly coat them.

⇒ On a foil-lined baking sheet, spread the ingredients in an equal layer.

⇒ Bake for 8 minutes, and serve hot.

8.11 Lobster Rolls Low-Carb

Preparation time: 20 minutes

Servings: 2

Nutrition Facts per Serving: Calories: 260, Carbohydrates: 24g, Sugar: 9g, Protein: 18g, Fat: 12g

Ingredients:

◊   1 tablespoon of unsalted butter melted

◊   2 teaspoons of lemon juice

◊   ¼ teaspoon of salt (optional)*

◊   1 tablespoon of olive oil mayonnaise

◊   12 ounces of cooked lobster

◊   2 large romaine lettuce

◊   2 tablespoons of plain non-fat Greek yogurt

◊   1 tablespoon of fresh chives, chopped

◊   ¼ teaspoon of black pepper (optional)*

◊   1 stalk of celery, finely chopped

◊   ¼ teaspoon of old bay seasoning

Instructions:

⇒ Preheat the grill or the oven broiler at 400°F.

⇒ To make a boat-like shape for the lobster filling, cut romaine lettuce hearts in ½ lengthwise and remove a few inner leaves from each side.

⇒ Brush the insides and edges of each "boat" with butter, then grill or broil to gently sear the lettuce and bring out the flavors. (maximum 2 to 3 minutes)

⇒ Combine all other ingredients in the medium-sized mixing bowl, except the lobster meat.

⇒ Toss in the lobster flesh until it is fully covered after all of the ingredients have been well mixed.

⇒ Serve immediately by dividing the lobster mixture equally among the boats and garnishing it with a lemon slice before serving.

8.12 Shrimp with Cauliflower Grits

Preparation time: 20 minutes

Servings: 2

Nutrition Facts per Serving: Calories: 245, Carbohydrates: 9g, Sugar: 2g, Protein: 26g, Fat: 11g

Ingredients:

◊   ½ tablespoon of Cajun seasoning

◊   1 tablespoon of unsalted butter

◊   1/8 teaspoon of salt (optional)*

◊   1 tablespoon of lemon juice

◊   1/3 cup of low-fat cheddar cheese shredded

◊   2 cups of frozen riced cauliflower

◊   ¼ cup of scallions, sliced

◊   12 ounces of shrimp

◊   Light cooking spray

◊   ¼ cup of low sodium chicken broth

◊   ½ cup of unsweetened almond milk

◊   2 tablespoons of light sour cream

Instructions:

⇒ In a large-sized resealable plastic bag, combine the shrimp with Cajun spice. Close the plastic bag and toss the shrimp to coat them with spices evenly.

⇒ Cook over a medium flame in a medium-sized skillet sprayed with cooking spray. Cook the shrimp until they are pink on both sides, approximately 2 to 3 minutes on each side. Simmer for 1 minute with lemon juice and chicken stock, scraping any pieces from the bottom of the pan, then put aside.

⇒ Melt butter in a separate skillet over a medium flame. Cook for 5 minutes after adding the riced cauliflower. Cook for another 5 minutes after adding the milk and salt.

⇒ Remove from the flame and whisk in the sour cream and cheese until they are completely melted.

⇒ Serve the shrimp over cauliflower grits with scallions on top.

8.13 Salmon Florentine

Preparation time: 25 minutes

Servings: 2

Nutrition Facts per Serving: Calories: 310, Carbohydrates: 11g, Sugar: 3g, Protein: 23g, Fat: 19g

Ingredients:

◊   1 small garlic clove, minced

◊   ¼ teaspoon of crushed red pepper flakes

- ◊ ½ cup of green onions, chopped
- ◊ ¼ teaspoon of black pepper
- ◊ Light cooking spray
- ◊ 1 teaspoon of olive oil
- ◊ 1 cup of spinach, chopped
- ◊ 6 ounces of salmon
- ◊ 1 ½ cup of cherry tomatoes, chopped
- ◊ 1/8 teaspoon of salt (optional)*
- ◊ ½ cup of ricotta cheese

Instructions:

⇒ Preheat the oven to 350 °F.

⇒ Cook onions in oil in a medium-sized pan until they soften, approximately 3 minutes.

⇒ Cook for another minute after adding the garlic. A

⇒ dd the chopped cherry tomatoes, salt (optional), crushed red pepper flakes, and pepper to the spinach.

⇒ Cook for 2 minutes, stirring occasionally.

⇒ Remove from flame and set aside for 10- 15 minutes to cool.

⇒ Add the ricotta cheese and mix well.

⇒ Top each salmon fillet with a quarter of the spinach mixture.

⇒ Bake for 15 minutes on a lightly oiled rimmed baking sheet.

⇒ Serve immediately.

8.14 Pan Seared Zucchini and Scallops with Red Pepper Sauce

Preparation time: 20 minutes

Servings: 2

Nutrition Facts per Serving: Calories: 212, Carbohydrates: 13g, Sugar: 3g, Protein: 22g, Fat: 8g

Ingredients:

- ◊ ½ cup of unsweetened almond milk
- ◊ 1 small garlic clove
- ◊ Light cooking spray
- ◊ ½ Avocado
- ◊ ¼ + 1/8 teaspoons of salt
- ◊ ½ cup of roasted red peppers
- ◊ 2 teaspoons of lemon juice
- ◊ 1 cup zucchinis
- ◊ 12 ounces of scallops

Instructions:

⇒ Add the (drained) roasted red pepper, milk, avocado, crushed red pepper, lemon juice, garlic, and ¼ teaspoon of salt to a blender or a food processor. Puree until completely smooth.

⇒ In a pan, cook roasted red pepper sauce over a medium flame, stirring periodically, until well heated, approximately 3 to 5 minutes.

⇒ Add the zucchini noodles, mix to combine, and simmer for another 3 to 5 minutes, or until cooked to your satisfaction.

⇒ Meanwhile, spray a large-sized pan on a medium-high flame—season scallops with the rest of the salt (optional).

⇒ Cook scallops for 1 to 2 minutes until golden brown on both sides and transparent in the middle.

⇒ Serve scallops over zucchini noodles.

8.15 Shrimp and Avocado Cauliflower Rice Sushi

Preparation time: 20 minutes

Servings: 2

Nutrition Facts per Serving: Calories: 232, Carbohydrates: 12g, Sugar: 4g, Protein: 27g, Fat: 9g

Ingredients:

- ◊ 1 tablespoon of rice vinegar
- ◊ 2 teaspoons of sriracha
- ◊ 12 ounces of shrimp, chopped
- ◊ ½ medium sliced cucumber
- ◊ 1 ½ cups of frozen riced cauliflower
- ◊ 2 (sheets) of large Nori
- ◊ 1/8 teaspoon of zero-calorie sugar substitute
- ◊ 1/3 cup of plain non-fat Greek yogurt
- ◊ ½ medium avocado
- ◊ 1 tablespoon of sesame seeds

Instructions:

⇒ Microwave cauli "rice" for about 5 minutes in a medium microwave-safe bowl, stirring halfway through. Set aside after adding the rice vinegar and sugar replacement.

⇒ Mix in chopped shrimp, Greek yogurt, and sriracha.

⇒ Assemble the sushi rolls; Place one sheet of nor on a rolling sushi mat and evenly distribute one-quarter of the cauliflower rice mixture over ½ of the sheet closest to you.

⇒ Place the contents horizontally over the cauliflower rice, leaving some cauliflower rice exposed both behind and in front of them (two slices of avocado, one sliced cucumber, and one quarter shrimp mixture per roll).

⇒ Roll the sushi by tucking the contents into the first full roll by folding the edges of exposed nori closest to you all over the filling. Roll till you reach the end of the nori sheet.

⇒ Replace the nori sheets, cauliflower rice, and fillings with the remaining nori sheets, cauliflower rice, and fillings. Cut the rolls into pieces with a sharp knife.

⇒ Sprinkle sesame seeds on top and serve.

8.16 Salmon Burger with Cucumber Salad

Preparation time: 20 minutes

Servings: 2

Nutrition Facts per Serving: Calories: 238, Carbohydrates: 16g, Sugar: 5g, Protein: 17g, Fat: 10g

Ingredients:

- 1 ½ tablespoons of light mayonnaise
- ¼ teaspoon of dried parsley
- 7 ounces of canned pink salmon
- 2 tablespoons of plain non-fat Greek yogurt
- 1 dash of Black Pepper
- ½ teaspoon of Dried Dill
- 1 large egg beaten
- ½ teaspoon of lemon juice
- 1 packet of multigrain crackers crushed
- 1 tablespoon of onion, minced
- 2 cups of cucumber sliced

- 1 dash of black pepper
- light cooking spray
- 2 tablespoons of apple cider vinegar

Instructions:

⇒ Combine the yogurt, vinegar, dill, salt (optional), and pepper in a mixing bowl.

⇒ Add thinly sliced cucumbers and toss to incorporate. Refrigerate until ready to serve.

⇒ Meanwhile, whisk the light mayo, egg, lemon juice, chopped onion, dry parsley, and pepper in a small-sized bowl.

⇒ Fold in the crackers and salmon.

⇒ Make two patties by dividing the ingredients in half and half.

⇒ In a lightly oiled pan on a medium-high flame, cook for approximately 5 minutes on each side.

⇒ Serve the hot salmon burgers with cold cucumber salad.

8.17 Shrimp Cauli Rice

Preparation time: 30 minutes

Servings: 2

Nutrition Facts per Serving: Calories: 316, Carbohydrates: 11g, Sugar: 4g, Protein: 29g, Fat: 17g

Ingredients:

◊ 2 egg whites beaten

◊ 2 small garlic cloves, minced

◊ ½ cup of green bell peppers, diced

◊ 2 tablespoons of canola oil

◊ 1 cup of frozen riced cauliflower

◊ 12 ounces of raw shrimp

◊ ¼ teaspoon of black pepper

◊ 1 large egg beaten

◊ ¼ teaspoon of salt (optional)*

◊ 2 tablespoons of low sodium soy sauce

◊ 1 stalk of scallions, minced

◊ ½ cup of green beans, chopped

Instructions:

⇒ Heat one tablespoon of canola oil over a medium-high flame in a wok or nonstick skillet. Scramble the egg in the skillet.

⇒ Remove from the flame and season with salt and black pepper (optional).

⇒ Heat the remaining canola oil in the wok or skillet. Cook for 2 minutes until the garlic and scallions are fragrant.

⇒ Cook for 2 minutes after adding the shrimp (raw, peeled, and deveined).

⇒ Add the bell pepper and green beans and cook for another 5 minutes.

⇒ Toss in the cauliflower with soy sauce. After the shrimp and veggies have finished cooking, mix in the scrambled eggs and serve immediately.

8.18 Blackened Shrimp in Lettuce Wraps

Preparation time: 30 minutes

Servings: 2

Nutrition Facts per Serving: Calories: 459, Carbohydrates: 43g, Sugar: 18g, Protein: 39g, Fat: 14g

Ingredients:

◊ 1 tablespoon of Old Bay Seasoning

◊ ¼ cup of green bell peppers, finely diced

◊ 2 tablespoons of lime juice, divided

◊ 1 medium jalapeno pepper, finely chopped

◊ ¼ cup of plain non-fat Greek yogurt

◊ ¼ cup of fresh cilantro, chopped

◊ 4 (Leaves) large romaine lettuce

◊ 12 ounces of raw shrimp

◊ 2 teaspoons of olive oil, divided

◊ ½ avocado

◊ ¼ cup of tomatoes, diced

Instructions:

⇒ Combine the shrimp and Old Bay seasoning in a resealable plastic bag.

⇒ Shake the contents of the bag to distribute the seasoning properly.

⇒ Heat the oil in a large nostick skillet and add 1/2 of the shrimp in a single layer. Cook for 3

minutes on each side. Rep with the remaining shrimp and olive oil.

⇒ In a blender or food processor, combine Greek yogurt, avocado, and one tablespoon of lime juice for the avocado crema. Blend until completely smooth.

⇒ Combine the tomatoes, green bell pepper, jalapeño pepper, cilantro, and the remaining tablespoon of lime juice in a mixing bowl.

⇒ Divide the shrimp, tomato, and salsa avocado crema equally among the lettuce leaves to make the lettuce wraps.

⇒ Serve right away.

8.19 Grilled Cajun-Flavored Catfish

Preparation time: 20 minutes

Servings: 2

Nutrition Facts per Serving: Calories: 105, Carbohydrates: 1g, Sugar: 0.1g, Protein: 12g, Fat: 5g

Ingredients:

◊ ½ teaspoons of thyme leaves

◊ ¼ teaspoon of garlic powder

◊ 14 ounces of raw wild catfish

◊ ¼ teaspoon of red cayenne pepper

◊ ¼ teaspoon of lemon pepper

◊ ½ teaspoon of black pepper

◊ ¼ teaspoon of onion powder

◊ ¼ teaspoon of salt

Instructions:

⇒ Preheat the oven to 375°F or set the grill at High

⇒ In a small-sized bowl, combine the spices, then sprinkle over the catfish.

⇒ Grill on for 5 minutes on each side or until the fish readily flakes.

⇒ Alternatively, you may bake it for 8 to 12 minutes or until the salmon flakes easily.

⇒ Serve immediately.

8.20 Super Easy Fish Tacos

Preparation time: 20 minutes

Servings: 2

Nutrition Facts per Serving: Calories: 238, Carbohydrates: 3g, Sugar: 1g, Protein: 15g, Fat: 19g

Ingredients:

◊   ½ teaspoon of ground cumin

◊   14 ounces of raw tilapia

◊   ½ teaspoon of chili powder

◊   ¼ teaspoon of salt

◊   ¼ teaspoon of black pepper

◊   For the toppings:

◊   4 tablespoons of approved dressing of choice

◊   2 teaspoons of lime juice

◊   ¼ avocado

Instructions:

⇒   Preheat the oven to 375 °F.

⇒   Line a baking sheet with baking paper. Season the tilapia on both sides with salt, pepper, cumin, and chili powder.

⇒   Bake for 20 to 25 minutes, or until done.

⇒   To hold the cooked fish, place each 7-ounce piece on romaine lettuce—1 teaspoon of lime juice and 2 tablespoons of dressing drizzled over each portion.

⇒   Serve with avocado or 2 tablespoons of sour cream

8.21 Fire Cracker Shrimps

Preparation time: 15 minutes

Servings: 2

Nutrition Facts per Serving: Calories: 204, Carbohydrates: 13g, Sugar: 9g, Protein: 28g, Fat: 4g

Ingredients:

◊   2 tablespoons of Walden Farms apricot preserves

◊   ½ teaspoon of sriracha sauce

◊   14 ounces of raw, peeled shrimp

◊   1 teaspoon of sesame oil

◊   1 teaspoon of lite soy sauce

Instructions:

⇒   Preheat the grill to medium heat.

⇒   Microwave the apricot preserves into a small-sized dish for 20 seconds or until they are partly melted.

⇒   Toss the melted apricot preserves with the sriracha sauce, soy sauce, and oil, and mix until well blended.

⇒   With a metal or wet wooden skewer, thread shrimp onto the skewer.

⇒   Brush both sides of the shrimp with the sauce. Before grilling, let the shrimp marinate in the sauce for approximately an hour.

⇒   Grill for 2 to 3 minutes on each side, uncovered, over medium heat.

⇒   Serve right away.

8.22 Cajun Flavored Skillet Shrimp

Preparation time: 15 minutes

Servings: 2

Nutrition Facts per Serving: Calories: 262, Carbohydrates: 10g, Sugar: 4g, Protein: 24g, Fat: 13g

Ingredients:

◊   1 ¼ teaspoons of Cajun seasoning

◊   ½ cup of canned Great Value Italian diced tomatoes

◊   1 tablespoon of light butter

◊   1 teaspoon of garlic, minced

◊   2 cups of frozen cauliflower rice

◊   1 tablespoon of olive oil

◊   14 ounces of raw shrimp, shells and tails removed

◊   ½ cup of assorted bell peppers, chopped

Instructions:

⇒   Melt the butter and oil in a large-sized pan over a medium-high flame.

⇒   Add the garlic and cook for 1 minute before adding the shrimp.

⇒   Sprinkle the Cajun spice over the shrimp and simmer for approximately 4 minutes, or until they are fully cooked.

⇒   In a large nonstick pan, cook bell peppers, chopped tomatoes, and cauliflower rice for about 10 minutes.

⇒   Add the shrimp to the veggie pan and simmer for 1 minute.

⇒   Serve hot and enjoy.

8.23 Sea Scallops Broiled

Preparation time: 15 minutes

Servings: 2

Nutrition Facts per Serving: Calories: 186, Carbohydrates: 6g, Sugar: 0g, Protein: 19g, Fat: 9g

Ingredients:

◊ 1 tablespoon of Land O' Lakes light spreadable butter with canola oil

◊ ¼ teaspoon of onion powder

◊ 1/8 teaspoon of ground cayenne pepper

◊ 9 ounces of dry sea scallops

◊ ¼ teaspoon of paprika

◊ ¼ teaspoon of garlic powder

◊ 1 teaspoon of olive oil

◊ ¼ teaspoon of salt

Instructions:

⇒ In a small-sized bowl, combine the spices.

⇒ Toss the scallops in the seasoning to cover both sides.

⇒ In a separate small dish, combine the olive oil with butter. Stir up the butter and olive oil mixture and pour it over the scallops.

⇒ Scallops should be placed on a broiler pan. Broil for 12-14 minutes on high, rotating every 4 to 5 minutes. When done, the scallops must be milky white or opaque and solid. Make sure they aren't overcooked, or they will become rubbery.

⇒ Serve immediately with your favorite veggies.

8.24 Quick and Easy Shrimp Risotto

Preparation time: 15 minutes

Servings: 2

Nutrition Facts per Serving: Calories: 178, Carbohydrates: 6g, Sugar: 2g, Protein: 17g, Fat: 9g

Ingredients:

◊ 1 tablespoon of low-fat grated Kraft Parmesan cheese

◊ 1/8 teaspoon of black pepper

◊ 1 tablespoon of Land O' Lakes light butter spread with canola oil

◊ 2 tablespoons of Philadelphia light cream cheese

◊ ½ teaspoon of dried parsley flakes

◊ ¼ teaspoon of salt

◊ 1 teaspoon of garlic, minced

◊ 7 ounces of peeled, tails removed and cooked shrimp

◊ 1 ½ cups of grated cooked cauliflower

Instructions:

⇒ Melt the butter in a medium-sized pan, add garlic, and sauté for 1 minute over a medium-high flame.

⇒ Reduce the flame to medium and add in the cream cheese. Stir well until combined.

⇒ Add the cream cheese mixture to the shrimp, grated cauliflower, salt, Parmesan cheese, and pepper. Stir until everything is well mixed.

⇒ Cook for 5 minutes over medium flame.

⇒ Garnish with parsley flakes and serve.

8.25 Grilled Shrimp Marinated

Preparation time: 15 minutes

Servings: 2

Nutrition Facts per Serving: Calories: 203, Carbohydrates: 2g, Sugar: 1g, Protein: 28g, Fat: 9g

Ingredients:

◊ 1 tablespoon of red wine vinegar

◊ 1 clove of garlic, minced

◊ 1/8 teaspoon of cayenne pepper

◊ 1 tablespoon + 1 teaspoon of olive oil

◊ 14 ounces of fresh shrimp, peeled and deveined

◊ 2 tablespoons of Rao's marinara sauce

◊ 1 tablespoon of fresh basil, chopped

◊ Skewers

◊ ¼ teaspoon of salt

Instructions:

⇒ In a large-sized mixing bowl, combine the garlic, tomato sauce, olive oil, and red wine vinegar.

⇒ Add salt, basil, and cayenne pepper. Stir the shrimp in the dish until they are uniformly covered. Refrigerate for 30 minutes to 1 hour, stirring every 30 minutes as so.

⇒ Preheat the grill to medium.

⇒ Thread the shrimp onto skewers, piercing them once near the tail and once near the head. Remove the marinade and discard it.

⇒ Grease the grill grate lightly—Cook shrimp for 2 to 3 minutes on each side on a hot grill or until opaque.

⇒ Serve immediately.

8.26 Pan Seared Cajun Flavored Tilapia

Preparation time: 15 minutes

Servings: 2

Nutrition Facts per Serving: Calories: 129, Carbohydrates: 1g, Sugar: 0g, Protein: 15g, Fat: 7g

Ingredients:

◊ 1 teaspoons of olive oil

◊ ¼ teaspoon of garlic powder

◊ 14 ounces of raw tilapia

◊ ¼ teaspoon of lemon pepper

◊ 1 teaspoon of Cajun seasoning

◊ 1 tablespoons of light butter

◊ ½ teaspoon of dried oregano

◊ ½ teaspoon of parsley flakes

Instructions:

⇒ Season the tilapia with spices.

⇒ In a large-sized skillet, melt the oil and butter over a medium flame.

⇒ Adjust the flame to medium-high and add the fish. The fish will be ready in no time. Cook for 2-3 minutes on each side, or until golden brown.

⇒ Serve immediately.

8.27 Peppers Stuffed with Jicama Tuna Salad

Preparation time: 15 minutes

Servings: 2

Nutrition Facts per Serving: Calories: 240, Carbohydrates: 5g, Sugar: 10g, Protein: 24g, Fat: 12g

Ingredients:

◊ 2 tablespoons of fresh cilantro, finely chopped

◊ 7 ounces of canned tuna, drained

◊ ¼ cup of celery, chopped

◊ 1 bell pepper sliced in ½ lengthwise, top and membrane removed

◊ 1 ½ tablespoon of light mayo

◊ 1/8 teaspoon of fresh ground black pepper

◊ ¼ teaspoon of Trader Joe's chili lime seasoning

◊ 2 slices of low-fat Provolone cheese slices

◊ 1 teaspoon of Dijon mustard

◊ ¼ cup of jicama, chopped

◊ 1 teaspoon of lime juice

Instructions:

⇒ Drain the tuna can and shred it with a fork in a small-sized mixing dish.

⇒ Mix in the mayonnaise, lime juice, chili-lime spice, Dijon mustard, and black pepper. Toss in the cilantro and celery.

⇒ Stuff the tuna mixture into the two pepper halves.

⇒ Place a piece of provolone cheese on each side.

⇒ Broil for 5 minutes. If you like the peppers soft rather than crispy, boil them for 5 minutes or until they reach the required softness.

⇒ Serve immediately.

8.28 Jambalaya Soup

Preparation time: 25 minutes

Servings: 2

Nutrition Facts per Serving: Calories: 172, Carbohydrates: 5g, Sugar: 2g, Protein: 19g, Fat: 8g

Ingredients:

◊ ½ cup of chicken broth

◊ ¼ teaspoon of Cajun seasoning

◊ 1 teaspoon of olive oil

◊ ¼ teaspoon of paprika

◊ ¼ cup of sweet bell pepper ˜ any color, chopped

◊ ½ cup of Italian diced tomatoes ˜ less than 5g carbs per serving

◊ ¼ cup of celery, chopped

◊ ¼ teaspoon of dried basil

◊ ½ cup of cauliflower rice, fresh or frozen

◊ 1 link of Alfresco andouille chicken sausage, sliced

◊ ¼ teaspoon of dried oregano leaves

◊ ½ teaspoon of garlic, minced

◊ 5 ounces raw shrimp, peeled and deveined

Instructions:

⇒ Heat olive oil in a medium-sized non-stick pan over a medium flame.

⇒ Simmer the peppers and celery until soft, approximately 4 to 5 minutes.

⇒ Add the sausage and cook until brown, another 5 minutes.

⇒ Add the garlic and cook for a few seconds to combine the flavors.

⇒ Add tomatoes, chicken broth, riced cauliflower, basil, Cajun spice, paprika, oregano, and shrimp.

⇒ Bring to a boil, then reduce to a low flame and cook for 5 to 7 minutes, or until the shrimp is cooked thoroughly and the cauliflower rice is soft.

⇒ Serve immediately.

8.29 Italian-Style Baked Tilapia

Preparation time: 25 minutes

Servings: 2

Nutrition Facts per Serving: Calories: 99, Carbohydrates: 3g, Sugar: 2g, Protein: 16g, Fat: 2g

Ingredients:

◊ ½ cup of Great Value Italian diced tomatoes, canned

◊ ¼ teaspoon of garlic powder

◊ 14 ounces of raw tilapia

◊ ¼ cup of green pepper, chopped

◊ 2 tablespoons of Ken's Steakhouse Lite Northern Italian with basil and Romano

◊ 1/8 teaspoon of pepper

◊ 1 tablespoon of grated reduced-fat Parmesan cheese

◊ ¼ teaspoon of salt

Instructions:

⇒ Preheat the oven to 350°F.

⇒ Drizzle dressing over tilapia in a baking dish lined using nonstick foil or coated with nonstick cooking spray.

⇒ Season with salt, pepper, and garlic powder. Tomatoes should be spooned over the fish, and green peppers should be sprinkled on top.

⇒ Cover and bake for about 30 minutes at 350°F. Remove the lid and top with Parmesan cheese. Cook for another 5 minutes. Serve hot and enjoy.

8.30 Grilled Ginger Lemon Shrimp

Preparation time: 25 minutes

Servings: 2

Nutrition Facts per Serving: Calories: 260, Carbohydrates: 2g, Sugar: 0.5g, Protein: 35g, Fat: 11g

Ingredients:

◊ 1 teaspoon of sesame oil

◊ 2 tablespoons of fresh cilantro

◊ 18 ounces of shrimp, peeled, tails removed and deveined

◊ ½ teaspoon of ground ginger

◊ 1 tablespoon of olive oil

◊ ¼ teaspoon of paprika

◊ 1 tablespoon + 2 teaspoons of lemon juice

◊ ¼ teaspoon of salt

◊ ¼ teaspoon of garlic powder

◊ Skewers

Instructions:

⇒ Combine the olive oil, lemon juice, sesame oil, garlic, paprika, ginger, cilantro, and salt in a medium-sized mixing bowl.

⇒ Toss in the prawns and toss to coat. Refrigerate for 2 hours after covering.

⇒ Preheat the grill to medium.

⇒ With skewers, thread shrimp onto them, piercing them once near the tail and the head. Remove the marinade and discard it.

⇒ Grease the grill grate lightly. Cook 3 minutes on each side on the grill or until opaque.

⇒ Serve hot and enjoy.

8.31 Shrimp Vegetable Quiche

Preparation time: 40 minutes

Servings: 2

Nutrition Facts per Serving: Calories: 158, Carbohydrates: 7g, Sugar: 4g, Protein: 22g, Fat: 4g

Ingredients:

◊   ½ cup of egg beaters

◊   5 ounces of shrimp, cooked and tails removed

◊   1/8 teaspoon of black pepper

◊   1 tablespoon of low-fat Parmesan cheese

◊   ½ cup of canned Italian diced tomatoes, drained

◊   ¼ cup of low-fat shredded cheddar cheese

◊   1 cup of zucchini, chopped

◊   ½ teaspoon of Mrs. Dash garlic and herb or salt-free seasoning of choice

◊   2 light laughing cow cheese wedges

Instructions:

⇒   Preheat the oven to 375 °F.

⇒   Coat a casserole dish with light cooking spray.

⇒   In a mixing dish, combine all the ingredients (except for the Parmesan). Pour into the casserole that has been prepared.

⇒   Bake for 30-35 minutes.

⇒   Sprinkle with Parmesan cheese and serve hot.

8.32 Tasty Shrimp Salad with Peanut Butter Dressing

Preparation time: 20 minutes

Servings: 2

Nutrition Facts per Serving: Calories: 178, Carbohydrates: 7g, Sugar: 3g, Protein: 23g, Fat: 6g

Ingredients:

◊   10 ounces of cooked shrimp, tails and shells removed

◊   1 ½ cups of tri-color coleslaw mix

For the dressing:

◊   ½ packet of stevia or to taste

◊   2 tablespoons of powdered peanut butter

◊   1/8 teaspoon of crushed red pepper

◊   1 ½ tablespoons of water

◊   ¼ teaspoon of ground ginger

◊   2 teaspoons of sesame oil

◊   2 teaspoons of lite soy sauce

Instructions:

⇒   In a medium-sized mixing bowl, combine the coleslaw mix and shrimp.

⇒   In a small-sized mixing bowl, combine all of the peanut dressing ingredients.

⇒   Pour the sauce over the shrimp and vegetables.

⇒   Toss to coat evenly. Enjoy!

8.33 Healthy Shrimp Lo Mein

Preparation time: 15 minutes

Servings: 2

Nutrition Facts per Serving: Calories: 146, Carbohydrates: 6g, Sugar: 2g, Protein: 20g, Fat: 4g

Ingredients:

◊   ½ cup of broccoli

◊   ¼ teaspoon of ground ginger

◊   ½ cup of spaghetti squash cooked

◊   1 teaspoon of olive oil

◊   ¼ teaspoon of garlic powder

◊   1 tablespoon of lite soy sauce

◊   1 teaspoon of teriyaki sauce

◊   12 ounces of raw shrimp, deveined and tails off

Instructions:

⇒   Heat the oils over a medium-high flame in a wok or a large nonstick skillet.

⇒   Add shrimp and for about 3 minutes.

⇒   Add the spaghetti squash, broccoli, sauces, and seasonings. Toss until everything is evenly covered.

⇒   Cook for ten more minutes over a medium flame.

⇒   Serve and enjoy!

9.1 Tofu Power Bowl

Preparation time: 30 minutes

Servings: 2

Nutrition Facts per Serving: Calories: 332, Carbohydrates: 13g, Sugar: 4g, Protein: 31g, Fat: 17g

This recipe is vegetarian-friendly

Ingredients:

◊   ½ cup of eggplant cubed

◊   ½ cup kale, chopped

◊   20 ounces of extra firm Tofu

◊   2 tablespoons of low sodium soy sauce

◊   1 teaspoon of sesame oil

◊   ½ cup of cauliflower grated

◊   1 teaspoon of rice vinegar

Instructions:

⇒   Tofu should be pressed. Place tofu strips on top of a plate or chopping board and cover with several layers of paper towels or (cheesecloth). On top of the tofu, add another layer of paper towels, clean dish towels, or another clean dish towel. On top of the second layer, place a weight. Let tofu rest for at least 15 minutes before cutting into 1-inch cubes.

⇒   In a large-sized skillet, heat the sesame oil. On the opposite side, arrange the cubed eggplant. Cook for 10 to 12 minutes, or until both are gently browned and soft. Remove the pan from the flame and put it aside. Sauté the kale, soy sauce, with rice vinegar until wilted, about 3 to 5 minutes.

⇒   In a small microwave-safe dish, microwave the grated cauliflower for 3 to 4 minutes, or until soft.

⇒   In a bowl, combine cauliflower "rice," tofu, eggplant, and kale.

9.2 One-Pan Shakshuka

Preparation time: 20 minutes

Servings: 2

Nutrition Facts per Serving: Calories: 190, Carbohydrates: 5g, Sugar: 1g, Protein: 14g, Fat: 12g

This recipe is vegetarian-friendly

Ingredients:

◊   1 stalk of scallions, minced

- ◊ ½ teaspoon of paprika
- ◊ 1 tablespoon of low-fat feta
- ◊ ¼ teaspoon of black pepper
- ◊ ¼ cup of tomatoes. diced
- ◊ 1 teaspoon of canola oil
- ◊ ½ cup of fresh cilantro, chopped
- ◊ 1 medium garlic clove, minced
- ◊ ¼ cup red bell peppers, chopped
- ◊ 1 teaspoon of cumin crushed
- ◊ 4 large eggs
- ◊ ¼ teaspoon of salt (optional)*

Instructions:

⇒ In a cast iron or nonstick skillet, heat 1 tablespoon of canola oil on a low flame. Add the scallions, garlic, and bell pepper and cook, often turning, for about 2 minutes or until transparent.

⇒ Combine cumin, of chopped tomatoes, and paprika. Cook for another 5 minutes after bringing the contents to a simmer.

⇒ To make a well in the tomato mixture, push the back of a tablespoon into it. Each time you make a well, break an egg and pour it into the indentation, continuing until you have 12 wells.

⇒ Cover and simmer for another 5 minutes, or until the egg, whites look firm after you've finished filling the 12 wells with eggs.

⇒ Remove the skillet from the flame and sprinkle the eggs with crumbled feta and chopped fresh cilantro. It must be served hot.

9.3 Tofu Vegan Stroganoff with Mushrooms

Preparation time: 25 minutes

Servings: 2

Nutrition Facts per Serving: Calories: 425, Carbohydrates: 20g, Sugar: 6g, Protein: 40g, Fat: 20g

This recipe is vegetarian-friendly

Ingredients:

- ◊ 1 medium garlic clove, minced

- ◊ 1 tablespoon of low sodium soy sauce
- ◊ 1 cup of zucchini
- ◊ 25 ounces of extra firm tofu sliced
- ◊ ¼ teaspoon of salt (optional)*
- ◊ 1 cup of cremini mushrooms sliced
- ◊ ½ cup of yellow squash
- ◊ 1 stalk of scallions, diced
- ◊ 1 ½ cup of vegetable stock
- ◊ 1 stalk of fresh thyme
- ◊ 2 tablespoons of light sour cream
- ◊ ¼ teaspoon of black pepper (optional)*

Instructions:

⇒ Shred the zucchini and/or yellow squash into broad noodles using a vegetable peeler, mandolin, or spiralizer. Set them aside.

⇒ Combine the garlic, stock, scallions (trimmed/sliced), tofu, thyme, veggie stock, soy sauce, and mushrooms. Simmer for 5 to 8 minutes, or until mushrooms are soft.

⇒ While they are cooking, bring a saucepan of water to a boil and blanch the zucchini and/or yellow squash for 2 to 5 minutes. Drain thoroughly.

⇒ Stir in the sour cream after removing the tofu mixture from the flame. If desired, season with salt and black pepper.

⇒ Serve the stroganoff over pappardelle made from zucchini or yellow squash.

9.4 Veggie Egg Tofu Bowls

Preparation time: 30 minutes

Servings: 2

Nutrition Facts per Serving: Calories: 372, Carbohydrates: 12g, Sugar: 4g, Protein: 30g, Fat: 22g

This recipe is vegetarian-friendly

Ingredients:

- ◊ 2 teaspoons of canola oil
- ◊ ¼ cup red bell peppers, diced
- ◊ 10 ounces of extra firm tofu

◊   ¼ cup of Roma tomatoes, diced

◊   ¼ teaspoon of salt (optional)*

◊   2 small garlic cloves, minced

◊   ½ teaspoon of black pepper

◊   4 large eggs

◊   ¼ cup Cauliflower Florets

◊   ¼ cup of button mushroom, halved

◊   ¼ cup of yellow squash, diced

◊   1 teaspoon of Sirach

◊   1 tablespoon of fresh ginger root, minced

◊   2 tablespoons of low-fat Parmesan cheese

◊   1 tablespoon of low-sodium soy sauce

◊   ¼ cup of fresh cilantro, crushed

Instructions:

⇒   Cut the tofu into cubes after patting it dry. Season with salt and black pepper, if desired. Heat the 2 tablespoons of oil in a large-sized saucepan or wok over a medium-high flame and sear the tofu on both sides until golden brown; put aside.

⇒   In a large-sized saucepan or wok, combine the cauliflower, mushrooms, tomatoes, peppers (seeds removed), squash, ginger (finely chopped), Sirach, garlic, soy sauce, and 2 cups water.

⇒   Bring to a boil on high flame with the tofu on top. Reduce flame to medium-high and cook for 12 to 15 minutes, stirring occasionally.

⇒   Reduce flame to medium-low and, using a slotted spoon or skimmer, scoop out all of the veggies and tofu into 4 serving dishes, dividing evenly.

⇒   Carefully crack the eggs into the leftover boiling liquid, making sure they don't break. Cook for 5 minutes on low flame.

⇒   Remove the eggs from the liquid with a slotted spoon and place one egg on top of each vegetable and tofu dish.

⇒   Pour an equal quantity of cooking liquid over each dish and stir in the cilantro (coarsely chopped).

⇒   Serve immediately with a ½ spoonful of Parmesan cheese sprinkled on top of each bowl.

9.5 Green Bean Lasagna

Preparation time: 35 minutes

Servings: 2

Nutrition Facts per Serving: Calories: 387, Carbohydrates: 20g, Sugar: 5g, Protein: 30g, Fat: 20g

This recipe is vegetarian-friendly

Ingredients:

◊   2 tablespoons of Rao's marinara sauce

◊   2 cups of green beans

◊   ½ teaspoon of basil

◊   2 cups of part-skim ricotta cheese

◊   1 tablespoon of low-fat Parmesan cheese

◊   ¼ teaspoon of garlic salt

Instructions:

⇒   Green beans should be prepared and placed in a baking dish.

⇒   Combine the ricotta cheese, garlic salt, and basil in a mixing bowl. Pour the mixture over the green beans.

⇒   On top of the ricotta cheese mixture, spread marinara sauce.

⇒   Bake for 15 minutes at 350 °F, then broil until the cheese is gently browned.

⇒   Top with a sprinkling of Parmesan cheese and serve.

9.6 Instant Pot Kimchi and Napa Cabbage Stew

Preparation time: 30 minutes

Servings: 2

Nutrition Facts per Serving: Calories: 183, Carbohydrates: 15g, Sugar: 3g, Protein: 18g, Fat: 9g

This recipe is vegetarian-friendly

Ingredients:

◊   ¼ cup of kimchi, chopped

◊   ¼ cup of white vinegar

◊   2 tablespoons of Korean chili flakes

- ◊ 14 ounces of soft tofu drained
- ◊ 1 cup of Napa cabbage
- ◊ 3 cups of water
- ◊ 2 small garlic cloves, minced
- ◊ ½ cup of kimchi juice
- ◊ 2 large eggs (optional)*
- ◊ 2 stalks of scallions sliced

Instructions:

⇒ On the Instant Pot, press the sauté button. Cook 5 minutes after adding cabbage, garlic, kimchi (no sugar added), and Korean chili flakes or (paprika).

⇒ Combine the vinegar, kimchi juice, and water. Secure the cover, change the setting to stew, and set the timer to 10 minutes.

⇒ Whenever the Instant Pot beeps, let the pressure out normally. Open the cover and crack one egg at a time into the pan. Cook the eggs to desired consistency by pressing the sauté button one more. (If you want, leave out the eggs.)

⇒ Cut tofu into tiny cubes after draining and drying it with a paper towel or cloth. Cook for a few more minutes after adding the tofu to the stew.

⇒ Serve in dishes with scallions on top.

9.7 Portobello Mushroom Pizza

Preparation time: 20 minutes

Servings: 2

Nutrition Facts per Serving: Calories: 180, Carbohydrates: 7g, Sugar: 3g, Protein: 16g, Fat: 9g

This recipe is vegetarian-friendly

Ingredients:

- ◊ ¼ cup of Rao's homemade sauce
- ◊ 2 tablespoons of fresh basil, chopped
- ◊ 2 large Portobello mushroom caps
- ◊ 4 ounces of reduced-fat cheese, shredded

Instructions:

⇒ Preheat the oven to broil.

⇒ Arrange the mushroom caps on a foil-lined baking sheet that has been gently oiled.

⇒ Coat the tops with nonstick cooking spray. Broil for 3 to 4 minutes on each side under the broiler until tender.

⇒ Distribute the tomato sauce evenly in each cup, then top with the cheese and basil. Broil for another 2 to 3 minutes, or until the cheese is completely melted.

9.8 Mexican-Style Bell Pepper Casserole

Preparation time: 50 minutes

Servings: 2

Nutrition Facts per Serving: Calories: 395, Carbohydrates: 13g, Sugar: 6g, Protein: 43g, Fat: 18g

This recipe is vegetarian-friendly

Ingredients:

- ◊ ½ cup of plain non-fat Greek yogurt
- ◊ 1 teaspoon of olive oil
- ◊ ½ teaspoon of dry mustard
- ◊ 2 medium green bell peppers, chopped
- ◊ 3 large eggs
- ◊ ½ cup of onion sliced
- ◊ 1 teaspoon of cumin
- ◊ ¼ teaspoon of cayenne pepper
- ◊ 1 small garlic clove, minced
- ◊ ¼ teaspoon of salt
- ◊ ½ teaspoon of coriander
- ◊ 8 ounces of low-fat cheddar cheese shredded

Instructions:

⇒ Preheat the oven to 375 °F.

⇒ Combine the eggs and yogurt in a mixing bowl and set it aside.

⇒ Cook onions and garlic in oil with spices in a medium-sized pan until onions are transparent.

⇒ Cook, occasionally stirring, for 4 to 5 minutes if using frozen peppers and 8 to 10 minutes if using fresh peppers on low flame.

⇒ Spread half of the pepper mixture and top with half of the cheese; repeat the layering into a deep casserole dish. Over the top, pour the yogurt mixture.

⇒ Bake for 30 minutes covered, then uncover and bake for another 15 minutes.

9.9 Vegan Meatballs with Zucchini Noodles

Preparation time: 20 minutes

Servings: 2

Nutrition Facts per Serving: Calories: 395, Carbohydrates: 13g, Sugar: 6g, Protein: 43g, Fat: 18g

This recipe is vegetarian-friendly

Ingredients:

◊ 2 cups zucchini spiraled

◊ ¼ cup of fresh basil, chopped

◊ 12 ounces of vegan meatballs

◊ 1 cup of Rao's homemade sauce

◊ 2 tablespoons of olive oil

Instructions:

⇒ Vegan meatballs should be heated as directed on the package, either in the oven or in the microwave.

⇒ In a pan, heat the olive oil on a medium-high flame. Stir zucchini noodles to the heated olive oil and toss until softened, about 2-3 minutes.

⇒ Reduce the flame to low and toss the zucchini noodles with Rao's Homemade Sauce. Boil for 3 minutes.

⇒ Before serving, add the cooked meatballs to the sauce noodle combination and heat for another 2 minutes. Serve with a fresh basil garnish on top of each serving.

9.10 Tasty Broccoli Salad

Preparation time: 20 minutes

Servings: 2

Nutrition Facts per Serving: Calories: 161, Carbohydrates: 13g, Sugar: 3g, Protein: 13g, Fat: 8g

This recipe is vegetarian-friendly

Ingredients:

◊ 2 tablespoons of low-fat mayo

◊ ¼ teaspoon of salt, optional

◊ 2 cups of broccoli florets

◊ 2 tablespoons of sliced almonds

◊ ¼ cup of 2% plain Greek yogurt

◊ 1 packets of stevia

◊ 1/3 cup of low-fat shredded cheddar cheese

◊ 1 tablespoon of apple cider vinegar

◊ 2 tablespoons of low sodium vegan bacon bits

Instructions:

⇒ Set aside cleaned broccoli florets in a medium-sized mixing dish.

⇒ Combine yoghurt, mayonnaise, vinegar, sweetener, and salt in a small-sized mixing dish. Stir until the mixture is completely smooth.

⇒ Pour the yogurt mixture over the broccoli and toss to incorporate everything. Combine the bacon, sliced almonds, bacon, and cheese. Gently toss until all of the pieces are equally covered.

9.11 Easy Cheese Broccoli Soup

Preparation time: 25 minutes

Servings: 2

Nutrition Facts per Serving: Calories: 144, Carbohydrates: 11g, Sugar: 5g, Protein: 15g, Fat: 5g

This recipe is vegetarian-friendly

Ingredients:

◊ 2 cups of vegetable broth

◊ 1/8 teaspoon of pepper

◊ ½ cup of low-fat shredded cheddar cheese

◊ 1/8 teaspoon of salt

◊ 2 cups of broccoli, chopped

◊ 1/8 teaspoon of garlic powder

◊ 4 light laughing cow cheese wedges

Instructions:

⇒ Add chicken stock, broccoli, pepper, salt, and garlic powder to a medium-sized saucepan.

⇒ Bring to a low boil, then turn off the flame. Cook for 12-15 minutes, or until broccoli is tender. Stir in the laughing cow cheese until it melts.

⇒ To purée the soup, use an immersion blender (or a blender in tiny batches). Pour ¼ cup cheese into each of the two dishes.

9.12 Cheese Broccoli Casserole

Preparation time: 20 minutes

Servings: 2

Nutrition Facts per Serving: Calories: 149, Carbohydrates: 6g, Sugar: 2g, Protein: 18g, Fat: 6g

This recipe is vegetarian-friendly

Ingredients:

◊ 1 ½ cups of broccoli

◊ 2 tablespoons of grated low-fat Parmesan cheese

◊ ½ tablespoon of light butter

◊ ½ cup of egg beaters

◊ 2 tablespoons of 1% cottage cheese

◊ ½ cup of shredded low-fat cheddar cheese

◊ ½ teaspoon of Mrs. Dash garlic and herb seasoning

Instructions:

⇒ Preheat the oven to 425 °F.

⇒ Use parchment paper or spray a baking sheet with cooking spray. Combine the soup, seasonings, baking powder, and water in a mixing bowl. Form a circle with the batter on the prepared cookie sheet.

⇒ Cook for 5 minutes before flipping with a spatula. If you want to add the cheese after flipping, do so now. Return the bread to the oven for another 5 minutes.

⇒ Once the bread is done baking, sprinkle the laughing cow cheese on top and serve.

9.13 Cauliflower Avocado Rice

Preparation time: 20 minutes

Servings: 2

Nutrition Facts per Serving: Calories: 66, Carbohydrates: 6g, Sugar: 2g, Protein: 2g, Fat: 5g

This recipe is vegetarian-friendly

Ingredients:

◊ 2 teaspoons of fresh lime juice

◊ ¼ cup of cilantro, chopped

◊ ¼ teaspoon of salt

◊ 1 ½ cups of raw grated cauliflower

◊ 1 ½ ounces of avocado

◊ 1/8 teaspoon of garlic powder

◊ 1 teaspoon of Stacey Hawkins roasted garlic oil or olive oil

Instructions:

⇒ Avocados should be mashed with a fork in a small-sized dish.

⇒ Combine the lime juice, salt, garlic powder, and cilantro in a mixing bowl. Stir until everything is well mixed.

⇒ Continue mashing until the mixture is completely smooth. Set them aside.

⇒ In a medium-sized pan, heat 1 teaspoon of oil over a medium flame.

⇒ Cauliflower should be grated.

⇒ Cover the pan and steam for 10 minutes.

⇒ Cook, stirring periodically, for 5 to 8 minutes.

⇒ Toss the cauliflower with the avocado mixture.

⇒ Combine all of the ingredients until the cauliflower is uniformly covered. Heat to a high temperature.

9.14 Baked Cream of Cauliflower Soup

Preparation time: 30 minutes

Servings: 2

Nutrition Facts per Serving: Calories: 68, Carbohydrates: 6g, Sugar: 3g, Protein: 7g, Fat: 2g

This recipe is vegetarian-friendly

Ingredients:

◊ 2 tablespoons of low-fat cheddar cheese

◊ 1 ½ cups of fresh cauliflower

◊ 1/8 teaspoon of black pepper

◊ 1 cup of vegetable broth

◊ 1/8 teaspoon of salt

◊ 2 wedges light laughing cow cheese

◊ 1 tablespoon of fresh chives, chopped

Instructions:

⇒ In a medium-sized saucepan, combine the cauliflower and broth. Bring to a boil.

⇒ Reduce to a low flame, cover, and cook for 15 minutes, or until the cauliflower is very mushy and falling apart.

⇒ Remove from flame and purée until smooth using an immersion blender. Blend in the light laughing cow cheese, salt, and pepper until smooth.

⇒ Add cheddar cheese and chives to a large mixing bowl.

⇒ Maintain a warm temperature until ready to serve.

9.15 Cauliflower and Alfredo Sauce

Preparation time: 20 minutes

Servings: 2

Nutrition Facts per Serving: Calories: 219, Carbohydrates: 29g, Sugar: 9g, Protein: 7g, Fat: 9g

This recipe is vegetarian-friendly

Ingredients:

◊ 3 cups of cauliflower florets

◊ ¼ teaspoon of black pepper

◊ 1 tablespoon of garlic, minced

◊ ½ teaspoon of salt

◊ 1 tablespoon of Kraft grated Parmesan cheese

◊ 1 ½ cups of low-sodium vegetable or chicken broth

◊ 1 tablespoon of light Land O' Lakes butter with canola oil spread

◊ 1 ½ cups of water

◊ 2 tablespoons cup of unsweetened almond milk

Instructions:

⇒ In a large-sized nonstick pan, sauté garlic with butter on low flame. Cook, occasionally stirring, until the garlic is tender and aromatic but not browned. Set them aside.

⇒ In a large saucepan, bring the water or the broth to a boil. Cook for 7 to 10 minutes, or until cauliflower is fork-tender. Observe the cooking time on the back of the box if using frozen cauliflower. Draining is not recommended.

⇒ Transfer the cauliflower to a blender using a slotted spoon. In a blender, combine 1 cup of

the cooking liquid, the garlic/butter, almond milk, salt, pepper, and Parmesan cheese.

⇒ Grind or puree the sauce for a few minutes or until it is completely smooth.

⇒ Serve immediately!

9.16 Cauliflower Bread Sticks

Preparation time: 40 minutes

Servings: 2

Nutrition Facts per Serving: Calories: 232, Carbohydrates: 11g, Sugar: 4g, Protein: 22g, Fat: 14g

This recipe is vegetarian-friendly

Ingredients:

◊ ¼ cup of liquid egg substitute

◊ ¼ teaspoon of dried basil

◊ 1 cup of raw grated cauliflower

◊ 1/8 teaspoon of garlic salt

◊ 1 cup or 4 ounces shredded low-fat mozzarella cheese, divided

◊ ¼ teaspoon of dried oregano

◊ For the Marinara Sauce:

◊ ¼ cup of Rao's Marinara Sauce

◊ ½ cup of Great Value Italian diced tomatoes

Instructions:

⇒ In a small chopper, puree-diced Italian tomatoes. Set them aside.

⇒ Preheat the oven to 350 °F.

⇒ In a mixing bowl, combine the cauliflower, ¼ cup of egg replacement, and 3 oz. or 3/4 cup of shredded mozzarella.

⇒ Spray a 9 x 5 loaf pan with cooking spray and line it with parchment paper.

⇒ Pour the mixture into a 1 1/2-inch deep pan. (It's OK if the mixture doesn't completely cover the pan.) Bake for about 30 minutes or until firm. Lift the paper's edges and put the bread on the cookie sheet with the parchment.

⇒ Lift the edges of the dough off the paper with a spatula and turn the dough. Preheat the oven to 450°F and bake for another 15 minutes. Remove from the oven and cut strips through the set dough using a pizza cutter. Separate by a little amount.

⇒ Add ¼ cup of 2 percent low-fat mozzarella or three cheese blend, garlic salt, and Italian spices. Bake for another 10 minutes at 450°F until the cheese has melted. Serve with marinara sauce on the side.

9.17 Cauliflower Casserole

Preparation time: 1 hour 10 minutes

Servings: 2

Nutrition Facts per Serving: Calories: 475, Carbohydrates: 12g, Sugar: 6g, Protein: 58g, Fat: 21g

This recipe is vegetarian-friendly

Ingredients:

- 2 cups of cauliflower florets
- 16 ounces of egg whites or egg beaters
- 3 ounces of Jennie-o bulk turkey sausage, cooked
- ¾ cup egg whites
- ¼ cup of onion, chopped
- ½ teaspoon of Feast Mode Asiago Jalapeno Seasoning
- ¼ cup of unsweetened almond milk
- ¼ teaspoon of salt
- ¼ teaspoon of fresh ground black pepper
- 1 cup of 2% Mexican style shredded cheese

Instructions:

⇒ Preheat the oven to 350 °F.

⇒ Coat a 9 x 13-inch baking dish with cooking spray.

⇒ Brown turkey sausage in a large-sized pan over a medium-high flame.

⇒ Weigh out 8 ounces of cooked turkey sausage and return it to the pan using a food scale.

⇒ Sauté the cauliflower and onions until they are caramelized.

⇒ Feast Mode seasoning Jalapeno Asiago Seasonings of your choosing, such as salt and pepper.

⇒ In a baking dish that has been prepared, spread the sausage and cauliflower mixture.

⇒ One cup of shredded cheese is sprinkled over the top of cauliflower and sausage.

⇒ In a large-sized mixing bowl, whisk together the eggs, egg whites, and almond milk unsweetened.

⇒ Over the sausage, cauliflower, and cheese, pour the egg mixture.

⇒ Keep 1 cup of cheese and sprinkle on top.

⇒ Bake for 40–45 minutes, or until the eggs are firm.

⇒ Let cool for 5 minutes. If desired, garnish with green onions.

9.18 Roasted Curried Cauliflower

Preparation time: 35 minutes

Servings: 2

Nutrition Facts per Serving: Calories: 98, Carbohydrates: 6g, Sugar: 2g, Protein: 2.2g, Fat: 7g

This recipe is vegetarian-friendly

Ingredients:

◊ 1 teaspoon of curry powder

◊ 2 cups of raw cauliflower, make bite-sized florets

◊ ½ teaspoon of garlic salt

◊ 1 tablespoon of olive oil

◊ ½ teaspoon of smoked paprika

Instructions:

⇒ Preheat the oven to 425 °F. Line a baking pan with nonstick aluminum foil.

⇒ In a gallon Ziploc bag, mix the oil with cauliflower florets and shake until well blended. Make an effort to cover all of the florets with oil. Then, add the smoked paprika, curry powder, and garlic salt. Spread the spice mixture over the cauliflower florets and shake the bag until the spice mixture is evenly distributed.

⇒ Distribute the cauliflower florets on the baking sheet, and bake for about 25 minutes, stirring halfway cooking.

9.19 Roasted Cauliflower Soup

Preparation time: 50 minutes

Servings: 2

Nutrition Facts per Serving: Calories: 67, Carbohydrates: 9g, Sugar: 4g, Protein: 4g, Fat: 3g

This recipe is vegetarian-friendly

Ingredients:

◊   1 cup of vegetable broth

◊   1/8 teaspoon of garlic powder

◊   2 ½ cups of cauliflower florets

◊   ¼ cup of lite coconut milk

◊   1/8 teaspoon of onion powder

◊   ¼ teaspoon of curry powder

◊   ¼ teaspoon of cumin

◊   1/8 teaspoon of salt

◊   ½ cup of water

◊   Garnish: 1 tablespoon of cilantro, chopped

Instructions:

⇒   Preheat the oven to 450 °F.

⇒   Spray an 8x8"baking pan with cooking spray and place cauliflower florets.

⇒   Bake until browned and tender, approximately 25-30 minutes in the middle of the oven, tossing the florets periodically to ensure uniform cooking.

⇒   Combine broth, ½ cup of water, and roasted cauliflower in a small-sized pot. Combine the curry powder, onion powder, cumin, garlic powder, and salt in a large mixing bowl.

⇒   Bring to a boil, then reduce to a low flame and simmer for 15 minutes, covered. Add the coconut milk and mix well.

⇒   Blend until smooth with an immersion blender (or in batches with a normal blender). To get the required consistency, add more water.

⇒   Garnish with chopped cilantro and serve.

9.20 Cauliflower Salad

Preparation time: 50 minutes

Servings: 2

Nutrition Facts per Serving: Calories: 96, Carbohydrates: 9g, Sugar: 5g, Protein: 10g, Fat: 6g

This recipe is vegetarian-friendly

Ingredients:

◊   1/8 teaspoon of fresh black pepper

◊   1 ½ cups of cauliflower cooked

◊   2 teaspoons of Dijon mustard

◊   1/8 teaspoon of paprika

◊   2 hard-boiled eggs cooked, peeled and chopped

◊   1/8 teaspoon of salt

◊   ½ cup of 2% plain Greek yogurt

◊   2 pickle spears, chopped

Instructions:

⇒   Cook the cauliflower and cut it into tiny florets. In a medium-sized mixing bowl, combine all of the ingredients.

⇒   Combine the eggs and pickles.

⇒   Combine yogurt, Dijon mustard, pepper, salt, and paprika in a separate small bowl.

⇒   Toss with the cauliflower mixture to coat.

⇒   Refrigerate until ready to serve.

9.21 Kabocha Pumpkin Pie

Preparation time: 1 hour

Servings: 2

Nutrition Facts per Serving: Calories: 235, Carbohydrates: 13g, Sugar: 6g, Protein: 8g, Fat: 18g

This recipe is vegetarian-friendly

Ingredients:

◊   ½ teaspoon of ground cinnamon

◊   2 cups of roasted kabocha squash

◊   ½ teaspoon of maple or vanilla extract

◊   ¼ cup of unsweetened cashew or almond milk

◊   1 packet of stevia

◊   2 egg whites

◊   ½ teaspoon of pumpkin pie spice

◊   12 walnut halves

Instructions:

⇒   Preheat the oven to 400 °F.

⇒ Line a baking pan with aluminum foil. Put kabocha squash into the microwave for 1 to 2 minutes if the skin is too tough to cut, then cut in half.

⇒ Remove all of the seeds using a spoon. Before baking, you may cut or peel the skin off. Squash should be cut into wedges. Place the wedges in the pan that has been prepared. Using nonstick frying spray, coat the wedges. Bake for 30 minutes. Turn the squash over to the other Cook for 10 to 15 minutes, or until done.

⇒ Let cool for 30 minutes.

⇒ Peel off the skin using a knife after it has cooled.

⇒ To create pies, follow these steps: preheat the oven to 425 °F. 4 ramekins sprayed with nonstick cooking spray. In a blender, combine 2 cups of squash (without the skin) and the other ingredients (except the walnuts).

⇒ Blend until completely smooth. Fill ramekins halfway with the mixture. Bake for about 15 minutes in the oven.

⇒ Reduce the heat to 350 °F. Remove the ramekins from the oven and sprinkle the walnuts equally over each one. Add another 25 minutes to the baking time.

9.22 Enchilada Bowls

Preparation time: 50 minutes

Servings: 2

Nutrition Facts per Serving: Calories: 118, Carbohydrates: 8g, Sugar: 3g, Protein: 6g, Fat: 7g

This recipe is vegetarian-friendly

Ingredients:

◊ ½ cup of low-fat mozzarella cheese

◊ 2 cups spaghetti squash

◊ Olive oil cooking spray

◊ 3 tablespoons of red enchilada sauce

Instructions:

⇒ Preheat the oven to 375 °F. Spaghetti squash should be cut in ½ lengthwise, and the seeds scraped out using a spoon. Spray spaghetti squash with olive oil cooking spray and place on a baking sheet.

⇒ Place the spaghetti squash on the baking sheet cut side down. Preheat oven to 350°F and bake for 45 minutes, or until squash is soft.

⇒ Remove from the oven and set aside to cool. Scrape the flesh with a fork to make spaghetti-like strands. In a medium-sized bowl, measure out 1 ½ cups of spaghetti squash.

⇒ Stir in the enchilada sauce and melt the mozzarella cheese on top for approximately 30 seconds in the microwave.

9.23 Parmesan Garlic Zoodles

Preparation time: 20 minutes

Servings: 2

Nutrition Facts per Serving: Calories: 97, Carbohydrates: 4g, Sugar: 2g, Protein: 2.4g, Fat: 7g

This recipe is vegetarian-friendly

Ingredients:

◊ ¼ cup of cherry tomatoes, cut in ½

◊ ¼ teaspoon of dried basil or fresh basil

◊ 1 ¼ cups of spiralizer zucchini

◊ 1/8 teaspoon of salt

◊ 1 tablespoon of light butter, such as Land O' Lakes

◊ 1 tablespoon light butter with canola oil

◊ Dash of fresh ground pepper

◊ 1 clove of garlic, minced

◊ 1 tablespoon of Kraft grated Parmesan cheese

Instructions:

⇒ In a large-sized skillet, heat the oil over a medium flame.

⇒ Add garlic to melted butter and cook for 1 minute.

⇒ Combine the zucchini noodles and tomatoes.

⇒ Cook for 2 to 3 minutes, or until the vegetables are soft.

⇒ If you overcook the zucchini, it will get mushy.

⇒ Turn off the flame in the pan.

⇒ Toss in the basil and Parmesan cheese.

⇒ If desired, season with salt and black pepper.

9.24 Roasted Kabocha Soup

Preparation time: 50 minutes

Servings: 2

Nutrition Facts per Serving: Calories: 97, Carbohydrates: 15g, Sugar: 8g, Protein: 2g, Fat: 3g

This recipe is vegetarian-friendly

Ingredients:

◊ 1 ½ cups of unsweetened cashew milk

◊ ¼ teaspoon of onion powder

◊ 3 cups of roasted kabocha squash

◊ ½ teaspoon of dried parsley

◊ 2 cups of vegetable broth

◊ ½ teaspoon of garlic powder

◊ 1/8 teaspoon of black pepper

Instructions:

⇒ Combine all ingredients in a medium saucepan over medium-high heat.

⇒ Bring this mixture to a boil, then reduce to a low flame and cook for 10 to 15 minutes.

⇒ The flavors will mix as a result of the simmering.

⇒ Blend the ingredients in a blender until smooth.

⇒ Let cool for 10 minutes before serving.

9.25 Spaghetti Squash Lasagne Casserole

Preparation time: 50 minutes

Servings: 2

Nutrition Facts per Serving: Calories: 428, Carbohydrates: 19g, Sugar: 7g, Protein: 40g, Fat: 21g

This recipe is vegetarian-friendly

Ingredients:

◊ 2 tablespoons of low-fat grated Parmesan cheese

◊ 8 ounces of part skim ricotta cheese

◊ ¼ teaspoon of garlic powder

◊ 2 cups of cooked spaghetti squash

◊ 1/8 teaspoon of pepper

◊ 8 ounces low-fat mozzarella cheese, divided

◊ 2 tablespoons of egg beaters

◊ 1 cup of Great Value Italian diced tomatoes, divided

Instructions:

⇒ Preheat the oven to 400 °F. Prick the squash with a fork or a metal skewer, then roast for 45 to 50 minutes, or until tender when pressed.

⇒ Remove it from the oven and set it on the counter to cool.

⇒ When the squash is cold enough to handle, split it in half and scoop out the seeds. Scoop out the remainder of the squash with a fork or spoon and put it aside in a bowl.

⇒ Take 2 cups of spaghetti squash and put the remainder in the refrigerator. Garlic powder and black pepper to taste.

⇒ Combine ricotta, Parmesan, egg beaters, and 4 oz. or 1 cup of mozzarella cheese.

⇒ Preheat the oven to 375 °F. 1 cup of Italian chopped tomatoes, spread equally in the bottom of a 9-inch or 8-inch square casserole dish, Toss in the squash. Place the ricotta cheese mixture on top of the squash.

⇒ Add 1 cup of diced Italian cheese over the meat.

⇒ Bake for 30 minutes. Spread the remaining mozzarella cheese (1 cup) over the top and bake for another 20 minutes, or until the cheese is melted and gently browned.

⇒ Let rest for 10 minutes before serving.

9.26 Spaghetti Squash with Feta, Basil and Tomatoes

Preparation time: 1 hour

Servings: 2

Nutrition Facts per Serving: Calories: 197, Carbohydrates: 15g, Sugar: 7g, Protein: 7g, Fat: 13g

This recipe is vegetarian-friendly

Ingredients:

◊ 2 cloves of garlic, minced

◊ ¼ teaspoon of black pepper

◊ 2 cups of prepared spaghetti squash

◊ ¼ cup of fresh basil, chopped

◊ 4 teaspoons of olive oil

◊ ½ cup of low-fat feta cheese

◊ 1 tablespoon of onion, chopped

◊ 1 cup of cherry tomatoes, chopped

◊ ¼ teaspoon of salt

◊ 1 cup of zucchini, chopped

Instructions:

⇒ Preheat the oven to 400°F.

⇒ Place the spaghetti squash cut side down on a baking sheet and bake for 45 to 50 minutes until a sharp knife can be pushed into the squash with just a little resistance.

⇒ Remove the squash from the oven and put it aside to cool enough to handle. Scoop out the stringy pulp from inside the squash with a big spoon and set aside 3 cups. The remainder may be saved for later.

⇒ Meanwhile, in a pan over a medium flame, heat the oil. 2 to 3 minutes in oil, sauté garlic and onion. Combine the tomatoes and zucchini. Cook just until fully heated.

⇒ Combine the squash, sautéed veggies, and basil in a large-sized mixing bowl.

⇒ Divide into two halves. Add 2 tablespoons of feta cheese on top of each piece.

⇒ Warm the dish before serving.

9.27 Zoodles with Lemon Cream Sauce

Preparation time: 1 hour

Servings: 2

Nutrition Facts per Serving: Calories: 207, Carbohydrates: 13g, Sugar: 4g, Protein: 14g, Fat: 12g

This recipe is vegetarian-friendly

Ingredients:

◊ 2 teaspoons of lemon juice

◊ 1 tablespoon of lemon peel

◊ 2 cups of zucchini, peeled with a julienne peeler

◊ 1 teaspoon of olive oil

◊ 1/8 teaspoon of fresh ground black pepper

◊ ½ teaspoon of garlic, minced

◊ ¼ teaspoon of kosher salt

◊ 8 ounces part-skim ricotta cheese

◊ 1 ½ tablespoons of water

◊ ¼ cup of sliced cherry tomatoes

Instructions:

⇒ Heat olive oil in a large-sized sauté pan over a medium-high flame and add garlic. Cook for 30 seconds.

⇒ Stir in the lemon juice, cherry tomatoes, and 1 ½ teaspoons of water until the cheese is completely melted.

⇒ Salt and pepper to taste.

⇒ Cook for 2 to 3 minutes, until zucchini noodles, are wilted, turning to cover with sauce.

⇒ Stir in the ricotta cheese and cook for 1 minute, or until heated.

⇒ Sprinkle lemon peel on top and serve.

9.28 Stir-Fry Asian Green Bean

Preparation time: 25 minutes

Servings: 2

Nutrition Facts per Serving: Calories: 111, Carbohydrates: 14g, Sugar: 2g, Protein: 4g, Fat: 5g

This recipe is vegetarian-friendly

Ingredients:

◊ 2 teaspoons of Sesame Oil

◊ 2 cups of fresh green beans, cooked

◊ ¼ teaspoon of garlic powder

◊ ½ cup of low sodium vegetables broth

◊ 2 tablespoon of lite soy sauce

◊ 1/4 teaspoon of ground ginger

Instructions:

⇒ Microwave green beans for 4 to 5 minutes in a covered dish with ½ cup water. Drain.

⇒ For 1 minute, heat a skillet on a medium-high flame. Swirl in the sesame oil to evenly coat the bottom of the pan. Stir in the green beans and cook for 5 minutes.

⇒ Combine the chicken stock, garlic powder, soy sauce, and ginger in a large-sized mixing bowl. 1 minute of stirring

⇒ Cook for 2 minutes with the lid on the skillet.

⇒ Serve hot or warm.

9.29 Almondine Green Bean

Preparation time: 25 minutes

Servings: 2

Nutrition Facts per Serving: Calories: 109, Carbohydrates: 8g, Sugar: 3g, Protein: 3g, Fat: 7g

This recipe is vegetarian-friendly

Ingredients:

◊ 2 teaspoons of sesame oil

◊ 2 cups of fresh green beans, washed and trimmed

◊ 1 tablespoon of sliced almonds

◊ ¼ teaspoon of garlic salt

◊ 1 teaspoon of lemon juice

◊ Dash of fresh ground black pepper, if desired

Instructions:

⇒ Green beans should be cooked in a medium-sized pan. Just cover the green beans with water. Bring to a boil, then reduce to a simmer for 3 to 4 minutes. To halt the cooking process, drain the green beans and put them in an ice bath.

⇒ Preheat the oven to 400 °F. Place almonds on a baking sheet in a single layer and toast for about 5 minutes, or until fragrant and gently brown, taking care not to burn them. Remove the dish from the oven.

⇒ Return the drained green beans to the skillet and cook on low. Toss in the sesame oil, salt, pepper, and lemon juice to coat. Stir in the almonds and cook for a few minutes or until completely warmed.

9.30 Southern Style Green Beans

Preparation time: 25 minutes

Servings: 2

Nutrition Facts per Serving: Calories: 216, Carbohydrates: 20g, Sugar: 8g, Protein: 4g, Fat: 15g

This recipe is vegetarian-friendly

Ingredients:

◊ 1 tablespoon of onion, chopped

◊ 1 ½ cups of vegetable broth

◊ 2 cups of fresh green beans

◊ ½ teaspoon of garlic powder

◊ ¼ teaspoon of black pepper

◊ 6 slices of vegetarian bacon, cooked and crumbled

Instructions:

⇒ Green beans should be washed, cut off the ends, and cut into 1 ½ inch sections. Green beans should be added to the slow cooker.

⇒ In a small-sized nonstick pan over a medium flame, add 2 to 3 tablespoons of chicken stock or water and the onions. Cook, often stirring, for approximately 5 minutes or until the onion is translucent.

⇒ Stir in the onion, garlic powder, broth, vegetarian bacon, and pepper in the slow cooker until everything is well mixed.

⇒ Cook, covered, for about 4 hours on high or 6 hours on low, stirring halfway cooking.

9.31 Spinach and Cheddar Quiche

Preparation time: 55 minutes

Servings: 2

Nutrition Facts per Serving: Calories: 203, Carbohydrates: 11g, Sugar: 4g, Protein: 26g, Fat: 6g

This recipe is vegetarian-friendly

Ingredients:

◊ 1 ½ cups of cauliflower florets

◊ ¼ teaspoon of pepper

◊ 1 cup of unsweetened almond or cashew milk

◊ ¼ teaspoon of onion powder

◊ 4 eggs whites

◊ 1 cup of frozen chopped spinach, thawed and well-drained

◊ 1 tablespoon of low-fat feta cheese

◊ 4 ounces of reduced-fat cheddar cheese, shredded

◊ ¼ teaspoon of garlic powder

◊ ¼ teaspoon of salt

Instructions:

⇒ Preheat the oven to 350 °F.

⇒ Prepare cauliflower rice with a food processor or using a grater. If you use a food processor be careful not to over process it or it'll get almost pureed.

⇒ Spread the cauliflower "rice" on a baking sheet lined with baking paper and bake for 20 minutes. Remove from oven and allow to cool. After half an hour, squeeze cauliflower to remove excess moisture.

⇒ Whisk together egg whites, and unsweetened almond milk in a mixing bowl. Combine the cheddar cheese, the cooked spinach and cauliflower rice. Season with salt and black pepper, as well as garlic and onion powders and feta cheese.

⇒ Grease an 8-inch pie pan . Add the cauliflower mixture and bake for 5 minutes after the crust is centered on the pan.

⇒ Bake at 450°F for 25 minutes, or until the knife inserted in the middle comes out clean. Remove from oven and cool for 10 minutes in pie plate before slicing and serving.

9.32 Baked Turnip Wedges

Preparation time: 35 minutes

Servings: 2

Nutrition Facts per Serving: Calories: 51, Carbohydrates: 7g, Sugar: 4g, Protein: 1g, Fat: 2g

This recipe is vegetarian-friendly

Ingredients:

◊ 1 teaspoon of olive oil

◊ 1 ½ cups of turnips, cut into steak fries

◊ Sea salt and black pepper, and garlic powder to taste

Instructions:

⇒ Preheat the oven to 425 °F.

⇒ Combine the turnips, olive oil, and spices in a mixing bowl.

⇒ Place on a cookie sheet and bake for 30 minutes.

⇒ Serve hot or warm as a side dish.

9.33 Eggplant Kebabs with Charred Onion Salsa

Preparation time: 45 minutes

Servings: 2

This recipe is vegetarian-friendly

Ingredients:

◊ 1 tablespoon of pomegranate molasses

◊ ½ teaspoon of ground cinnamon

◊ 1 tablespoon of olive oil

◊ 1 large eggplant, sliced lengthways into ½ cm slices

◊ 1 tablespoon of ground cumin

◊ 1 tablespoon of Aleppo pepper flakes

Charred Onion Salsa:

◊ 2 garlic cloves crushed

◊ ½ tablespoon of dried chili flakes

◊ 1 medium onion, sliced into thick rounds

◊ 2 tablespoons of finely shredded mint leaves

◊ 2 tablespoons of olive oil

◊ Greek yogurt for serving

Instructions:

⇒ Fire up the grill. Meanwhile, season the eggplant slices with 1 tablespoon of salt on both sides. Allow 30 minutes to drain in a colander or sieve, then rinse and pat dry.

⇒ To prepare the salsa, roast the onion slices on direct fire on the grill for 8 minutes, or until gently charred from both sides (skewering them beforehand will help them stay firm). Chop finely and combine with the other salsa components, as well as some salt and black pepper. Set aside.

⇒ In a mixing bowl combine molasses, cinnamon, cumin, sumac, Aleppo pepper, and olive oil. Brush equally over the eggplant slices, then thread them onto six skewers in a concertina manner, compressing them firmly.

⇒ Cook for 15-20 minutes on the grill, rotating once or twice, or until tender and gently browned. Toss with the onion salsa and yogurt before serving.

10.1 Kabocha Yogurt Parfait

Preparation time: 30 minutes

Servings: 2

Nutrition Facts per Serving: Calories: 110, Carbohydrates: 20g, Sugar: 16g, Protein: 4g, Fat: 6g

This recipe is vegetarian-friendly

Ingredients:

◊ 2 tablespoons of Walden Farms maple walnut syrup

◊ ½ cup of low-fat plain Greek yogurt

◊ 1 kabocha squash, ½ cup cooked and mashed

◊ ½ teaspoon of Pumpkin Pie Spice

◊ 2 tablespoons of unsweetened almond milk

◊ ½ ounce of walnuts, chopped

Instructions:

⇒ Preheat the oven to 375°

⇒ Toast the walnuts: place them in a single layer on the baking sheet and bake for 5 to 10 minutes, checking often. Remove from the oven and set aside.

⇒ Half the kabocha squash and scoop out the seeds; put cut side down on a lightly oiled baking sheet or a sheet coated with nonstick foil.

⇒ Bake for about 60 minutes, or until vegetables are soft. Wait half an hour until the flesh is cold before touching it and scraping it out. Place the mixture in a small-sized bowl.

⇒ Combine ½ cup squash, maple syrup, pumpkin spice, and milk in a mixing bowl until smooth.

⇒ In the bottom of an 8-ounce glass, layer half of the squash.

⇒ Layer ¼ cup of Greek yogurt on top.

⇒ After that, the other half of the squash and, ¼ cup Greek yogurt.

⇒ Serve with walnuts on top.

10.2 Cinnamon Jicama Apples Baked

Preparation time: 30 minutes

Servings: 4

Nutrition Facts per Serving: Calories: 144, Carbohydrates: 15g, Sugar: 9g, Protein: 1g, Fat: 8g

This recipe is vegetarian-friendly

Ingredients:

◊   ¼ teaspoon of apple pie spice

◊   3 cups of jicama peeled and cubed or sliced thin

◊   3 packets of raw stevia

◊   3 tablespoons of light Land O' Lakes Butter with Canola Oil, melted

◊   ¼ teaspoon of ground cinnamon

◊   Optional toppings:

◊   2 tablespoons of fat-free Reddi whip

◊   2 tablespoons of Walden Farms caramel syrup

Instructions:

⇒   Preheat the oven to 350 °F.

⇒   In a medium-sized mixing bowl, combine jicama and melted butter. Stir in the apple pie spice, cinnamon, and stevia.

⇒   Pour the batter into a foil-lined baking pan.

⇒   Wrap foil around the dish and bake for 20 minutes. Remove the top and bake for another 15 minutes.

⇒   Serve hot or warm.

10.3 Crustless Pumpkin Pie

Preparation time: 50 minutes

Servings: 4

Nutrition Facts per Serving: Calories: 176, Carbohydrates: 8g, Sugar: 3g, Protein: 5g, Fat: 15g

This recipe is vegetarian-friendly

Ingredients:

◊   ½ teaspoon of ground cinnamon

◊   2 cups of roasted kabocha squash

◊   ½ teaspoon of maple or vanilla extract

◊   ¼ cup of unsweetened cashew or almond milk

◊   28 Walnut halves

◊   2 egg whites

◊   ½ teaspoon of pumpkin pie spice

◊   1 packet of Stevia

Instructions:

⇒   Preheat the oven to 425 °F.

⇒   Spray ramekins with nonstick frying spray.

⇒   In a blender, combine 2 cups of squash (without the skin) and the other ingredients (except the walnuts). Blend until completely smooth.

⇒   Fill ramekins halfway with the mixture and bake for 5 minutes.

⇒   Reduce heat to 350 °F. Remove the ramekins from the oven and sprinkle the walnuts equally over each one. Bake for 25 minutes, then serve.

10.4 Mock Coconut Pie

Preparation time: 1 hour

Servings: 2

Nutrition Facts per Serving: Calories: 84, Carbohydrates: 4g, Sugar: 1g, Protein: 3g, Fat: 6g

This recipe is vegetarian-friendly

Ingredients:

◊   1 tablespoon of light butter, melted

◊   1 cup of cooked and shredded spaghetti squash

◊   3 packets of stevia

◊   ¼ teaspoon of vanilla extract

◊   1 egg

◊   1 teaspoon of lemon juice

◊   ¼ teaspoon of coconut extract

◊   Dust of cinnamon

Instructions:

◊   Preheat the oven to 350 °F.

◊   Combine the stevia with egg in a mixing bowl and whisk until light and fluffy.

◊   Blend in the vanilla, lemon juice, and butter until smooth.

◊   In a blender, pulse the spaghetti squash a few times to obtain tiny strands that resemble a coconut. Add the spaghetti squash and mix well.

◊ Fill two ramekins halfway with the ingredients. If desired, sprinkle cinnamon on top. Bake for 40 to 45 minutes until a knife inserted in the middle comes out clean.

◊ Before serving, cool on a rack.

10.5 Sweet Mock Kugel

Preparation time: 1 hour

Servings: 6

Nutrition Facts per Serving: Calories: 126, Carbohydrates: 12g, Sugar: 5g, Protein: 12g, Fat: 4g

This recipe is vegetarian-friendly

Ingredients:

◊ ¼ teaspoon of nutmeg

◊ 6 cups of spaghetti squash strands, cooked

◊ ¼ cup of low-fat cream cheese, softened

◊ 8 packets stevia or sweetener of choice

◊ 1 ½ cups of 2% cottage cheese

◊ 1 teaspoon of cinnamon

◊ 1/8 teaspoon of salt

◊ 1 teaspoon of vanilla extract

◊ 2 whole eggs plus 4 egg whites

Instructions:

⇒ Preheat the oven to 375 °F.

⇒ First, you shall cut the squash in half lengthwise and scoop out all seeds with a spoon.

⇒ Place both pieces into a shallow baking dish, cut side down, and bake for 45 minutes.

⇒ Allow cooling slightly, then scrape the threads off the spaghetti squash with a fork. Place spaghetti squash into a large-sized mixing dish.

⇒ Add the sweetener, nutmeg, cinnamon, salt, vanilla extract, eggs, cream cheese, and cottage cheese to a blender. Pulse until completely smooth.

⇒ Combine the sauce with the spaghetti squash, then transfer everything on a casserole dish coated with cooking spray— Bake for 40 minutes.

⇒ Let chill for 15 minutes before serving.

10.6 Cheesecake Treat

Preparation time: 1 hour

Servings: 2

Nutrition Facts per Serving: Calories: 120, Carbohydrates: 7g, Sugar: 3g, Protein: 12g, Fat: 3g

This recipe is vegetarian-friendly

Ingredients:

◊ 2 teaspoons of lemon juice

◊ 1 cup of 1% cottage cheese

◊ 1 teaspoon of vanilla extract

◊ 1 egg

◊ 1 teaspoon of lemon zest

◊ 3 packets of Stevia

◊ 1/8 teaspoon of salt

Instructions:

⇒ Preheat the oven to 350 °F.

⇒ In a blender, combine all of the ingredients and pulse until smooth.

⇒ Pour the mixture into two ramekins.

⇒ Bake for 55 minutes or until the center is set.

⇒ Let cool thoroughly before serving.

10.7 Caramel Salted Jicama Salad

Preparation time: 30 minutes

Servings: 2

Nutrition Facts per Serving: Calories: 251, Carbohydrates: 18g, Sugar: 11g, Protein: 10g, Fat: 16g

This recipe is vegetarian-friendly

Ingredients:

◊ ½ teaspoon of vanilla extract

◊ 3 cups of raw jicama, peeled and chopped

◊ ½ teaspoon of coarse sea salt

◊ 1 ½ cups of 2% plain Fage Greek yogurt

◊ 3 tablespoons of Walden Farms caramel syrup, divided

◊ ½ teaspoon of ground cinnamon

◊ 28 walnut halves

◊ 1 packet stevia

Instructions:

⇒ Preheat the oven to 350°F

⇒ Toast the walnut halves in a single layer on a prepared baking sheet for about 7 minutes. Walnuts are ready once they have darkened a bit and have a toasty aroma.

⇒ Let cool before chopping and setting aside.

⇒ In a medium-sized mixing bowl, combine the chopped jicama, yogurt, one tablespoon of caramel syrup, vanilla extract, cinnamon, stevia, and half of the chopped walnuts. Stir the jicama until it is uniformly covered.

⇒ Pour the mixture into a serving dish. Drizzle 2 tablespoons of caramel syrup over the top, then sprinkle the remaining walnuts on top.

⇒ Add a pinch of salt to and serve right away.

10.8 Cashew and Cheese Flapjacks

Preparation time: 30 minutes

Servings: 4

Nutrition Facts per Serving: Calories: 263, Carbohydrates: 17g, Sugar: 1g, Protein: 14g, Fat: 15g

This recipe is vegetarian-friendly

Ingredients:

◊ 1 tablespoon of cashew, chopped

◊ 1 large lightly beaten free-range egg

◊ 1 cup of porridge oats

◊ 2 tablespoons of butter

◊ 1 medium-sized carrot

◊ 1 cup of grated reduced-fat cheddar cheese

Instructions:

⇒ Preheat the oven to 380°F.

⇒ In a medium-sized saucepan, melt the butter on a low flame, then stir in the cashews, oats, carrot, cheese, and egg after removing the butter from the flame.

⇒ Lightly grease an 8-inch-by-8-inch baking tray and bake the flapjacks for about 20 minutes.

⇒ Remove from the oven and let cool on a wire rack for 20 minutes before serving.

10.9 Raw Apple and Raspberry Tart

Preparation time: 15 minutes

Servings: 2

Nutrition Facts per Serving: Calories: 134, Carbohydrates: 18g, Sugar: 11g, Protein: 2g, Fat: 7g

This recipe is vegetarian-friendly

Ingredients:

◊ 1 tablespoon of pecan nuts

◊ 1 tablespoon of cashew nuts

◊ ½ teaspoon of ground cinnamon

◊ 1 tablespoon of raw almonds

◊ A handful of raspberries

◊ 1 cup of apples, cut lengthways

◊ 2 soft dried dates

Instructions:

⇒ Pulse the pecan nuts, almonds, and cashew nuts in a blender until finely ground.

⇒ Combine the dates and cinnamon in a blender until well mixed and evenly dispersed. To thoroughly integrate the ingredients, add four tablespoons of water to the blender.

⇒ Half-fill four loose-bottomed tartlet cases with the ingredients and press down.

⇒ Serve with apple slices on top and raspberry on the side.

10.10 Ricotta Cheesecake Muffins

Preparation time: 30 minutes

Servings: 6

Nutrition Facts per Serving: Calories: 221, Carbohydrates: 20g, Sugar: 2g, Protein: 7g, Fat: 13g

This recipe is vegetarian-friendly

Ingredients:

◊ ½ tablespoon of stevia

◊ 1 cup of fresh raspberries

For the cheesecakes:

◊ ½ cup of digestive biscuits

- ◊ 1 tablespoon of softened butter
- ◊ 1 tablespoon of stevia
- ◊ 1 cup of ricotta cheese
- ◊ 3 eggs
- ◊ 1 teaspoon of vanilla essence

Instructions:

⇒ Preheat the oven to 350°F.

⇒ Meanwhile, purée the raspberries with a bit of water and ½ tablespoon of stevia in a blender.

⇒ Lightly grease four ramekin plates or equivalent small containers.

⇒ Using the digestive biscuits, make crumbs. You may accomplish this by crushing them in a zipped bag with a rolling pin.

⇒ Mix the crumbs and butter well.

⇒ Add the ricotta, stevia sweetener, egg whites, and vanilla extract to a mixing bowl and whisk well.

⇒ Halfway fill the ramekin dishes with the mixture.

⇒ Bake the cheesecakes for about 20 minutes or until golden brown.

⇒ Serve with the raspberries and fruit coulis on top.

10.11 Tasty Fruit Pizza

Preparation time: 15 minutes

Servings: 2

Nutrition Facts per Serving: Calories: 200, Carbohydrates: 20g, Sugar: 6g, Protein: 2g, Fat: 9g

This recipe is vegetarian-friendly

Ingredients:

- ◊ 1 tablespoon of softened butter
- ◊ Several mints leave for decoration
- ◊ 1 cup of strawberries
- ◊ ½ cup of broken digestive biscuits
- ◊ 3 tablespoons of lemon curd

Instructions:

⇒ Line a loose-bottomed 15-cm cake pan using greaseproof paper and butter gently.

⇒ In a food processor, pulse the digestive biscuit pieces and butter until the biscuits are finely broken and evenly distributed.

⇒ Chill the mixture after smoothing the buttery biscuit foundation into an even layer with the back of a dessert spoon in the prepared cake pan.

⇒ After one hour, pour the lemon curd on top of the chilled foundation.

⇒ Cut each strawberry into four pieces and place it on top of the lemon curd.

⇒ Garnish with mint leaves just before serving.

10.12 Crunchy Oatcakes

Preparation time: 20 minutes

Servings: 4

Nutrition Facts per Serving: Calories: 84, Carbohydrates: 15g, Sugar: 1g, Protein: 3g, Fat: 2g

This recipe is vegetarian-friendly

Ingredients:

- ◊ 2 cups of warm water
- ◊ 2 tablespoons of almond flour
- ◊ 1 cup of fine Oatmeal
- ◊ 1 teaspoon of salt

Instructions:

⇒ Preheat the oven to 300°F.

⇒ In a mixing dish, combine the oats, flour, and salt.

⇒ Pour the heated water in slowly.

⇒ On a floured surface, roll out the dough and knead until it is ¼ inch thick.

⇒ Cook on a grill or in a pan after cutting into triangles.

⇒ 3-4 minutes in the oven, or until crisp.

10.13 Crunchy Oat Honey Cookies

Preparation time: 20 minutes

Servings: 4

Nutrition Facts per Serving: Calories: 146, Carbohydrates: 17g, Sugar: 4g, Protein: 3g, Fat: 9g

This recipe is vegetarian-friendly

Ingredients:

- ◊ 1 tablespoon of medium oatmeal

◊ 1 medium lightly beaten egg

◊ 1 tablespoon of runny honey

◊ 2 tablespoons of vegetable oil

◊ 1 teaspoon of vanilla extract

◊ 1 tablespoon of pumpkin seeds

◊ ½ cup of porridge oats

◊ 2 tablespoons of Stevia

Instructions:

⇒ Preheat the oven to 350°F.

⇒ Line an 8x8-inch baking pan with baking paper.

⇒ Combine the oatmeal, porridge oats, Stevia, egg, honey, vanilla essence, oil, and pumpkin seeds in a large-sized mixing dish.

⇒ Pour the mixture on the baking pan and smooth it out with a spatula.

⇒ Bake for about 10 minutes and let cool before serving.

10.14 Yummy Milk Pudding

Preparation time: 25 minutes

Servings: 4

Nutrition Facts per Serving: Calories: 211, Carbohydrates: 13g, Sugar: 9g, Protein: 1g, Fat: 17g

This recipe is vegetarian-friendly

Ingredients:

◊ 2 teaspoons of vegetable oil

◊ ½ cup of double cream

◊ 1 tablespoon of Stevia

◊ 2 tablespoons of buttermilk

◊ 1 teaspoon of agar-agar

◊ 1 ½ cup of almond milk

For the syrup:

◊ Juice of a blood orange

◊ ½ cup of boiling water

◊ 4 drops of rose water

◊ 2 tablespoons of Stevia

Instructions:

⇒ Combine the milk and buttermilk in a large-sized mixing bowl.

⇒ Grease four dariole molds with vegetable oil and put them on a tray.

⇒ Heat the double cream in a small-sized saucepan over a medium flame. Stir in the Stevia until it dissolves fully.

⇒ Increase the flame and continue to boil the cream for about 2 minutes.

⇒ Combine the agar-agar and cream mixture in a mixing bowl.

⇒ Pour the cream mixture over the milk and buttermilk in the dariole molds. Once the mixture has cooled down, place it in the fridge to chill for 3-4 hours or overnight.

⇒ To make the syrup, put the stevia, blood orange juice, boiling water, and rose water in a mixing dish.

⇒ Stir until the stevia has completely dissolved.

⇒ Turn the milk puddings out onto four plates by running a rough knife along the edges of the molds. Serve with syrup on top.

10.15 Pecan Pancakes

Preparation time: 25 minutes

Servings: 4

Nutrition Facts per Serving: Calories: 157, Carbohydrates: 15g, Sugar: 4g, Protein: 2g, Fat: 10g

This recipe is vegetarian-friendly

Ingredients:

◊ 1 tablespoon of tapioca flour

◊ ¼ cup of rice flour

◊ 1 cup of almond milk

◊ 2 tablespoons of coconut oil

◊ 1 large-sized egg

For the topping:

◊ 1 tablespoon of toasted pecans

◊ 2 tablespoons of liquid stevia

Instructions:

⇒ Combine the rice flour, eggs, tapioca flour, and almond milk in a food processor and pulse for 2 minutes.

⇒ Half-fill a jug with the smooth batter.

⇒ In a large-sized nonstick frying pan, heat ½ tablespoons of coconut oil for each pancake.

⇒ Pour 1/8 of the batter onto the pan and swirl it around to create a full-size pancake.

⇒ Cook for 2 minutes, or until the edges of the pancake are golden brown.

⇒ With a spatula, flip the pancake and cook the other side. The second side should just take a minute to cook. Make sure both sides are golden. Then, with the remaining pancakes, repeat the procedure.

⇒ Wrap the pancakes in foil and place them in a low-temperature oven to keep them warm.

⇒ To serve up, layer two pancakes each dish onto a dish. Drizzle liquid stevia on top of the pancakes and sprinkle nuts on top.

10.16 Banana Cookies

Preparation time: 25 minutes

Servings: 6

Nutrition Facts per Serving: Calories: 134, Carbohydrates: 13g, Sugar: 6g, Protein: 4g, Fat: 8g

This recipe is vegetarian-friendly

Ingredients:

◊ 1/3 cup of almond milk

◊ ½ teaspoon of baking powder

◊ 2 bananas ripe

◊ 1 cup of almond flour

Instructions:

⇒ Preheat the oven to 350 °F.

⇒ In a mixing bowl, peel and mash the bananas. Mix in the almond milk until it's completely mixed.

⇒ In a separate bowl, whisk together the flour and baking powder until the mixture is thick and smooth.

⇒ Using an ice cream scoop, dollop equal-sized blobs of batter (about 13) onto a baking sheet lined with parchment paper.

⇒ In the oven, bake the cookies for 10 to 15 minutes.

⇒ Let them cool for a few minutes before serving.

10.17 Peanut Butter Cookies

Preparation time: 15 minutes

Servings: 2

Nutrition Facts per Serving: Calories: 96, Carbohydrates: 13g, Sugar: 1g, Protein: 5g, Fat: 7g

This recipe is vegetarian-friendly

Ingredients:

◊ 2 tablespoons of Stevia

◊ 1 tablespoon of peanut butter, sugar-free

◊ 1 egg

◊ 1 tablespoon of almond flour

Instructions:

⇒ Preheat oven at 325 °F and line cookie sheets with parchment paper.

⇒ In a large-sized mixing bowl, whisk together the peanut butter, stevia, flour, and egg until thoroughly mixed.

⇒ Drop teaspoons of cookie batter onto the baking sheet, leaving at least ½ inch of space between the cookies' borders. Bake for 8-10 minutes.

10.18 Protein Mocha Balls

Preparation time: 20 minutes

Servings: 6

Nutrition Facts per Serving: Calories: 183, Carbohydrates: 16g, Sugar: 10g, Protein: 5g, Fat: 13g

This recipe is vegetarian-friendly

Ingredients:

◊ 1 teaspoons of chia seeds

◊ ½ cup of pitted dates soaked in hot water for 10 mins

◊ ½ cup of walnuts or almonds

◊ ½ cup of almond meal

◊ 1 tablespoon of instant coffee in ½ cup of boiling water

◊ 1 tablespoon of cocoa powder

Instructions:

⇒ Combine nuts, almond meal, and chia seeds in a food processor.

⇒ Blend in the cacao, coffee that has been dissolved, and dates until smooth.

⇒ Make balls with heaping tablespoons of the mixture and, if preferred, roll them in coconut.

⇒ Refrigerate or freeze for up to 10 days.

10.19 Protein Peanut Butter Cheesecake

Preparation time: 20 minutes

Servings: 4

Nutrition Facts per Serving: Calories: 268, Carbohydrates: 19g, Sugar: 11g, Protein: 16g, Fat: 17g

This recipe is vegetarian-friendly

Ingredients:

◊ 4 ounces of cream cheese, softened

◊ 1 scoop of peanut butter protein powder

◊ 1 tablespoon of Splenda

◊ 1 tablespoon of creamy natural peanut butter

◊ ½ teaspoon of vanilla extract

◊ ½ package of vanilla instant pudding mix sugar-free

◊ ½ cup of unsweetened almond milk

◊ 4 teaspoons of peanuts, chopped

◊ 4 tablespoons of light whipped cream

Instructions:

⇒ Mix all of the ingredients well in a mixer.

⇒ Refrigerate for 4-6 hours.

⇒ As a garnish, top with light whipped cream and chopped peanuts.

10.20 Coconut Cream Cheesecake

Preparation time: 1 hour 20 minutes

Servings: 4

Nutrition Facts per Serving: Calories: 216, Carbohydrates: 12g, Sugar: 3g, Protein: 10g, Fat: 17g

This recipe is vegetarian-friendly

Ingredients:

◊ ¼ teaspoon of vanilla extract

◊ 2 tablespoons of melted butter

◊ ½ cup of almond flour

◊ 2 tablespoons of Stevia

◊ ½ teaspoon of cinnamon

◊ 1 large egg

◊ ¼ cup of coconut milk

◊ 1 tablespoon of toasted coconut

◊ 5 ounces of fat-free cream cheese at room temperature

Instructions:

⇒ Preheat the oven to 350° F.

⇒ Combine the crust ingredients and press into the bottom of a spring form pan. Keep the filling chilled while preparing it.

⇒ In a large-sized mixing bowl, combine the filling ingredients, just until the mixture is completely smooth.

⇒ Fill the crust with the filling and bake for 15 minutes. Reduce the oven temperature to 250 °F and bake for another 10 minutes.

⇒ Refrigerate for 3 hours.

⇒ Run a knife down the edge of the spring form side of the cake to remove it.

⇒ Let cool completely before garnishing with toasted coconut.

10.21 Chia Pudding

Preparation time: 20 minutes

Servings: 4

Nutrition Facts per Serving: Calories: 134, Carbohydrates: 11g, Sugar: 2g, Protein: 4g, Fat: 8g

This recipe is vegetarian-friendly

Ingredients:

◊ 1 tablespoon of mini dark chocolate chips

◊ 2 cups of unsweetened almond milk

◊ 6 tablespoons of chia seeds

◊ 1 teaspoon of vanilla

◊ 1 teaspoon of natural peanut butter

◊ 1 tablespoon of sugar-free maple syrup

Instructions:

⇒ Combine the chia seeds, maple syrup, protein almond milk and vanilla. Close the lid, then shake the contents of a mason jar to mix them.

⇒ Refrigerate at least for 4 hours for it to set before serving.

10.22 Frozen Greek Yogurt Bites

Preparation time: 1 hour

Servings: 6

Nutrition Facts per Serving: Calories: 164, Carbohydrates: 12g, Sugar: 7g, Protein: 7g, Fat: 9g

This recipe is vegetarian-friendly

Ingredients:

◊ 1 scoop of vanilla protein powder

◊ ¼ cup of almond milk

◊ 1 teaspoon of vanilla extract

◊ 8 ounces of vanilla Greek yogurt

◊ 4 ounces of cream cheese

◊ 1 small box of instant vanilla pudding (sugar-free)

Instructions:

⇒ Combine all of the ingredients in a stand mixer and beat until frothy. A splash of almond milk may help soften it up if it's too stiff.

⇒ Drop teaspoons onto a parchment-lined pan or pipe to make beautiful patterns.

⇒ Freeze and enjoy.

⇒ Add flavored oils, water flavor packets, pureed fruit, or PB2 to change the taste!

10.23 Pumpkin Flavored Donuts

Preparation time: 30 minutes

Servings: 6

Nutrition Facts per Serving: Calories: 165, Carbohydrates: 15g, Sugar: 1g, Protein: 7g, Fat: 12g

This recipe is vegetarian-friendly

Ingredients:

◊ 4 tablespoons of stevia

◊ 1 tablespoon of melted coconut oil

◊ 1 cup of almond flour

◊ 1 scoop vanilla protein powder

◊ ¼ cup of pumpkin puree

◊ ½ teaspoon of pumpkin pie spice

◊ 1 teaspoon of vanilla

◊ ½ teaspoon of baking powder

◊ 1 egg

◊ ½ teaspoon of salt

◊ 2 tablespoons of sugar-free vanilla pudding mix

Instructions:

⇒ Combine flour, protein, Splenda, pie spice, baking powder, salt, and pudding mix in a large mixing dish.

⇒ Combine the remaining ingredients in a separate bowl.

⇒ Slowly combine the wet and dry components.

⇒ Fill your doughnut pan halfway with batter, then bake at 350°F for 15 minutes.

⇒ Roll the doughnuts with in a Splenda and cinnamon mixture.

10.24 Ginger Snaps

Preparation time: 20 minutes

Servings: 2

Nutrition Facts per Serving: Calories: 113, Carbohydrates: 11g, Sugar: 1g, Protein: 2g, Fat: 9g

This recipe is vegetarian-friendly

Ingredients:

◊ 1 teaspoon of pure vanilla extract

◊ 1 teaspoon of ginger, minced

◊ 1 tablespoon of soft pure vegetable margarine

◊ ½ teaspoon of grated nutmeg

◊ 1 tablespoon of Stevia

◊ 2 tablespoons of almond flour

◊ 1 tablespoon of stem ginger, chopped

◊ 2 tablespoons of unsweetened soya milk

◊ ½ teaspoon of baking powder

◊ 1 teaspoon of ground cinnamon

Instructions:

⇒ Preheat the oven to 380°F and line a baking sheet with parchment paper.

⇒ Combine the veggie margarine and stevia in a large-sized mixing bowl and beat until light and creamy. This assignment takes 3 to 4 minutes to complete.

⇒ Continue to beat in the vanilla extract.

⇒ Combine the almond flour, stem ginger, baking powder, nutmeg, ginger, cinnamon, and salt.

⇒ Add enough soya milk to make a soft dough, then shape the dough into balls.

⇒ Arrange the balls on the baking pans so that there is some space between them.

⇒ Bake for 10 minutes, or until golden brown and flattened for each ball.

⇒ Let cool on a cooling rack for 5 minutes before serving.

11.1 Cinnamon Flavored Bun Blondies

Preparation time: 25 minutes

Servings: 2

Nutrition Facts per Serving: Calories: 162, Carbohydrates: 4g, Sugar: 1g, Protein: 4g, Fat: 15g

This recipe is vegetarian-friendly

Ingredients:

◊ ½ teaspoon of baking Powder

◊ 3 tablespoons of Liquid Egg Substitute, divided

◊ ¼ cup of light cream cheese

◊ 4 sachets of Cinnamon Cream Cheese Swirl Cake

◊ 2/3 cup of cashew milk

◊ ½ teaspoon of vanilla extract

◊ ½ teaspoon of cinnamon

◊ 2/3 cup of unsweetened vanilla almond milk

◊ 2 tablespoons of unsalted butter melted

◊ 1 1/3 ounces of pecans, chopped

◊ 1-2 packets of zero-calorie sugar substitute

◊ Light cooking spray

Instructions:

⇒ Preheat the oven to 350 °F.

⇒ Combine the cinnamon, Cinnamon Cream Cheese Swirl Cake, and baking powder in a large-sized mixing bowl. Stir in the milk, butter, then 2 tablespoons of liquid egg whites until well mixed. Pecans should be folded in at this point.

⇒ Pour the batter into a bread loaf pan that has been gently oiled.

⇒ Mix cream cheese, vanilla extract, sugar substitute, and the remaining 1 tablespoon of egg white in a small mixing bowl until thoroughly mixed. Swirl the cream cheese mixture into the batter with a knife.

⇒ Bake for 18-20 minutes, or until the batter has set and is gently browned.

11.2 Peanut Butter Brownie Whoopie Pies

Preparation time: 25 minutes

Servings: 2

Nutrition Facts per Serving: Calories: 205, Carbohydrates: 6g, Sugar: 2g, Protein: 8g, Fat: 19g

This recipe is vegetarian-friendly

Ingredients:

◊ 3 tablespoons of egg whites

◊ 2 sachets of double chocolate brownie

◊ 1 teaspoon of vegetable oil

- ◊ ¼ teaspoon of baking powder
- ◊ Light cooking spray
- ◊ 6 tablespoons of almond milk unsweetened
- ◊ ¼ cup of peanut butter powdered

Instructions:

⇒ Preheat the oven to 350 °F.

⇒ Combine the double chocolate brownie mix, egg replacement, almond milk, baking powder, and oil in a medium-sized mixing dish and stir until a batter-kind of texture is achieved.

⇒ Divide the batter equally among the muffin pan that has been gently oiled. Bake for 18 to 20 minutes, until a toothpick pierced in the middle, comes out clear.

⇒ In the meanwhile, whisk together the powdered peanut butter and the remaining milk.

⇒ After the muffins have cooled, cut them in ½ horizontally. Fill the bottom ½ of every muffin with one spoonful of peanut butter filling, then top with other muffin halves and enjoy!

11.3 PB Brownie Ice Cream Sandwiches

Preparation time: 15 minutes

Servings: 2

Nutrition Facts per Serving: Calories: 149, Carbohydrates: 10g, Sugar: 6g, Protein: 4g, Fat: 8g

This recipe is vegetarian-friendly

Ingredients:

- ◊ 1 Peanut Butter Crunch Bar
- ◊ 2 tablespoons of PB2
- ◊ 1 Brownie Mix
- ◊ 2 tablespoons of cool whip
- ◊ 3 tablespoons of water
- ◊ 1 tablespoon of water

Instructions:

- ◊ For 20 seconds, melt 1 brownie and 1 peanut butter crunch. Mix with 3 tablespoons of water. Using cooking spray, coat a plate. Four spoonsful of dough should be placed on a dish. Keep for 2 minutes in the microwave.

- ◊ To make a paste, combine PB2 with water. Stir peanut butter to each cookie and then

spread 1 tablespoon of cool whip. Top with a peanut butter cookie and a dollop of whip cream.

◊ Place the filled cookies in a Ziploc bag and freeze them completely. Each cookie is equivalent to one meal.

11.4 Peanut Butter Crunch Bars

Preparation time: 15 minutes

Servings: 2

Nutrition Facts per Serving: Calories: 216, Carbohydrates: 7g, Sugar: 1g, Protein: 6g, Fat: 18g

This recipe is vegetarian-friendly

Ingredients:

- ◊ 3 sachets of peanut butter crunch bars
- ◊ 1 sachet of chocolate pudding

Instructions:

⇒ In a medium-sized mixing dish, prepare the pudding according to the package directions and put it aside.

⇒ Microwave the peanut butter crunch bars into a separate dish for approximately 20 seconds or until melted. Stir the melted crunch bars into the prepared pudding until everything is well mixed.

⇒ To create bars: pour the mixture onto a baking sheet coated with parchment paper and evenly spread to desired thickness. You may alternatively use four silicone muffin cup holders and equally divide the ingredients between them.

⇒ Freeze for a minimum of 2 hours. If frozen on a baking sheet, cut into equal pieces or peel out the silicone cup and enjoy!

11.5 Chocolate Crunch Cookies

Preparation time: 15 minutes

Servings: 2

Nutrition Facts per Serving: Calories: 160, Carbohydrates: 2g, Sugar: 1g, Protein: 3g, Fat: 15g

This recipe is vegetarian-friendly

Ingredients:

- ◊ 1 sachet of brownie mix
- ◊ 3 tablespoons of water
- ◊ 1 sachet of peanut butter chocolate crunch bar or crunch bar of your choice

Instructions:

◊ Set aside 3 tablespoons of brownie mix and 3 tablespoons of water after mixing them together.

◊ Microwave the crunch bar for about 20 seconds on high, or until it is slightly melted, on a plate.

◊ Blend the crunch bar into the brownie batter until it is completely smooth.

◊ Spoon the mixture into two ramekins or a dish gently coated with cooking spray.

◊ Cook 2 minutes in the microwave. Let cool for 5 minutes.

11.6 Haystacks

Preparation time: 15 minutes

Servings: 2

Nutrition Facts per Serving: Calories: 172, Carbohydrates: 12g, Sugar: 1g, Protein: 2g, Fat: 11g

This recipe is vegetarian-friendly

Ingredients:

◊ 3 tablespoons of water

◊ 1 sachet of hot cocoa or brownie mix

◊ 1 packet of stevia - optional

◊ 1 sachet of cinnamon pretzel sticks, crushed

◊ 2 tablespoons of PB2

Instructions:

◊ Set aside 3 tablespoons of brownie mix and 3 tablespoons of water after mixing them together.

◊ Microwave the crunch bar for 20 seconds on high, or until it is slightly melted, on a plate.

◊ Blend the crunch bar into the brownie batter until it is completely smooth.

◊ Spoon the mixture into two ramekins or a dish gently coated with cooking spray. Cook 2 minutes in the microwave.

◊ Let cool for 5 minutes before serving.

11.7 Chocolate Chip Coffee Cake Muffins

Preparation time: 25 minutes

Servings: 2

Nutrition Facts per Serving: Calories: 197, Carbohydrates: 5g, Sugar: 1g, Protein: 7g, Fat: 18g

This recipe is vegetarian-friendly

Ingredients:

◊ 1 packet of sachet of frothy cappuccino

◊ 1 tablespoon of egg beaters

◊ 1 packet of sachet of golden chocolate chip pancakes

◊ ¼ cup of water

◊ 1 packet of Stevia

◊ ¼ teaspoon of baking powder (½ Condiment)

◊ For cream cheese frosting:

◊ ½ packet of stevia

◊ 2 tablespoons of light cream cheese

Instructions:

⇒ Preheat the oven to 350°F

⇒ Combine the ingredients in a mixing bowl. Fill a four-inch round plastic microwavable dish. Microwave for 1 minute on high. Check for consistency every 45 seconds to 2 minutes. Eat as soon as possible.

⇒ Bake for 15 minutes.

11.8 Peanut Butter Fudge Balls

Preparation time: 25 minutes

Servings: 2

Nutrition Facts per Serving: Calories: 254, Carbohydrates: 13g, Sugar: 1g, Protein: 5g, Fat: 14g

This recipe is vegetarian-friendly

Ingredients:

◊ 1 sachet of chocolate pudding

◊ 2 tablespoons of water

◊ 1 sachet of chocolate shake/ hot cocoa

◊ 4 tablespoons of powdered peanut butter

◊ ¼ cup of unsweetened almond milk

Instructions:

◊ In a small-sized mixing dish, combine all of the ingredients.

◊ Make eight fudge balls. One meal is made up of four balls.

11.9 Mousse Treat

Preparation time: 15 minutes

Servings: 2

Nutrition Facts per Serving: Calories: 218, Carbohydrates: 2g, Sugar: 1g, Protein: 2g, Fat: 22g

This recipe is vegetarian-friendly

Ingredients:

◊ 1 packet of hot chocolate

◊ 2 tablespoons to ¼ cup of cold water

◊ ½ cup of pre-made sugar-free gelatin

◊ ¼ cup of crushed ice

◊ 1 tablespoon of light cream cheese

Instructions:

⇒ In a bullet blender, combine all of the ingredients.

⇒ It's got a wonderful thick creamy feel to it! Enjoy!

11.10 Tiramisu Milkshake

Preparation time: 5 minutes

Servings: 2

Nutrition Facts per Serving: Calories: 130, Carbohydrates: 5g, Sugar: 1g, Protein: 3g, Fat: 12g

This recipe is vegetarian-friendly

Ingredients:

◊ ½ cup of water

◊ 1 tablespoon of Walden Farms Chocolate Syrup

◊ 1 package of cappuccino

◊ ½ cup of crushed ice

Instructions:

◊ In a small blender, combine all of the ingredients and mix for approximately 15 seconds.

11.11 Cadbury Creme Eggs

Preparation time: 20 minutes

Servings: 2

Nutrition Facts per Serving: Calories: 214, Carbohydrates: 9g, Sugar: 1g, Protein: 2g, Fat: 16g

This recipe is vegetarian-friendly

Ingredients:

◊ 1 packet of hot chocolate

◊ 2 tablespoons of water

For crème of egg:

◊ 1 tablespoon of Walden Farms marshmallow crème

◊ 1 tablespoon of PB2

For outside of egg:

◊ 1 tablespoon of Walden Farms chocolate syrup

Instructions:

⇒ Blend the hot chocolate mix with 2 tablespoons of water until smooth. Form an oval shape with half of the mixture on a plate.

⇒ Combine the PB2 and marshmallow crème. There's no need to use any water. It's okay if the middle is a bit thick, as long as it's blended.

⇒ On top of the 1/2 oval form in the middle, place a spoon. Form an oval egg shape with the remaining half of the hot chocolate mixture. 1 tablespoon of chocolate syrup, spread on top of the egg.

⇒ Freeze for a minimum of 20 minutes.

11.12 Chocolate Peanut Butter Cups

Preparation time: 15 minutes

Servings: 2

Nutrition Facts per Serving: Calories: 112, Carbohydrates: 6g, Sugar: 1g, Protein: 3g, Fat: 10g

This recipe is vegetarian-friendly

Ingredients:

◊ 2 tablespoons of PB2

◊ 1 package of Hot Cocoa or brownie mix

◊   1 packet of stevia

Instructions:

◊   Stir together 2 tablespoons of peanut butter and stevia with water. Remove from the equation.

◊   Combine hot cocoa and 3 tablespoons of water in a separate container. Half of the mixture should be spread on top of the bottom of a ramekin.

◊   On the chocolate base layer, spread PB2. Cover the top of the PB2 with the remaining hot cocoa mixture.

◊   Place for at least 1 hour in the freezer before serving.

11.13 Bread Pudding

Preparation time: 35 minutes

Servings: 2

Nutrition Facts per Serving: Calories: 202, Carbohydrates: 8g, Sugar: 1g, Protein: 6g, Fat: 18g

This recipe is vegetarian-friendly

Ingredients:

◊   1 packet of stevia

◊   1 packet of maple and brown sugar oatmeal

◊   ¼ teaspoon of cinnamon

◊   2 tablespoons of Walden Farms caramel syrup

◊   1 packet of vanilla pudding

◊   3/4 cup of water

◊   1 teaspoon of vanilla extract

◊   ½ cup of egg beaters

◊   ¼ teaspoon of baking powder

Instructions:

⇒   Combine all ingredients and bake at 350°F for 30 minutes in a glass dish measuring 7 x 5 x 1.5 inches or a loaf pan.

⇒   Spread caramel syrup on top and enjoy!

11.14 Garlic Potato Pancakes

Preparation time: 15 minutes

Servings: 2

Nutrition Facts per Serving: Calories: 117, Carbohydrates: 5g, Sugar: 2g, Protein: 6g, Fat: 3g

This recipe is vegetarian-friendly

Ingredients:

◊   ¼ cup of low-fat cheese, optional

◊   1 packet of garlic mashed potatoes

◊   ¼ teaspoon of baking powder

◊   ½ cup of water

Instructions:

⇒   Combine the mashed potatoes, water, baking powder, and cheese in a large-sized mixing bowl. It should take about 5 minutes for the sauce to thicken up.

⇒   Using cooking spray, lightly coat a cast-iron skillet.

⇒   Preheat the skillet to medium-high flame.

⇒   Spoon the ingredients into two pancakes on the skillet.

⇒   Fry the pancakes for a few minutes before flipping them to cook on the other side.

⇒   Serve with 2 tablespoons of sour cream or a tablespoon of low sugar ketchup!

11.15 Coconut Chocolate Cake

Preparation time: 35 minutes

Servings: 2

Nutrition Facts per Serving: Calories: 232, Carbohydrates: 6g, Sugar: 3g, Protein: 7g, Fat: 21g

This recipe is vegetarian-friendly

Ingredients:

◊   1 packet of chocolate pudding

◊   1 teaspoon of coconut extract

◊   2 maple and brown sugar oatmeal's

◊   1 tablespoon of oil

◊   2 tablespoons of egg beaters

◊   3/4 to 1 cup of water

◊   1 teaspoon of baking powder

Instructions:

⇒   Preheat the oven to 350 °F.

⇒   Coat a baking dish with cooking spray.

⇒   In a medium-sized mixing dish, combine all of the ingredients and stir until well combined. Pour into the pan that has been prepared.

⇒   Bake for 22 minutes.

⇒ Use a toothpick to test the middle of your cake to see whether it has been set. It's finished if it comes out clean.

⇒ Turn the cake out onto a baking sheet. Bake for 10 minutes on the opposite side, or until the edges are crispy and golden.

11.16 Granola

Preparation time: 15 minutes

Servings: 2

Nutrition Facts per Serving: Calories: 270, Carbohydrates: 8g, Sugar: 1.2g, Protein: 9g, Fat: 24g

This recipe is vegetarian-friendly

Ingredients:

◊ 1 packet of stevia

◊ ¼ teaspoon of apple pie spice

◊ 1 package of oatmeal

◊ ½ teaspoon of vanilla extract

Instructions:

⇒ Preheat the oven to 400 °F.

⇒ Combine the ingredients in a mixing dish and add just enough water to make the granola stick together (about 3 to 4 tablespoons).

⇒ One by one, place onto a cookie sheet that has been coated using nonstick cooking spray. If required, separate the items.

⇒ Bake for about 8 minutes, then flip and bake for 3 to 4 minutes more. When it's done, It should be golden and crispy.

11.17 Maple Pancakes

Preparation time: 5 minutes

Servings: 2

Nutrition Facts per Serving: Calories: 181, Carbohydrates: 7g, Sugar: 1g, Protein: 5g, Fat: 15g

This recipe is vegetarian-friendly

Ingredients:

◊ ¼ teaspoon of baking powder

◊ 1 packet of stevia

◊ 1 packet of maple brown sugar oatmeal

◊ ¼ cup of water

◊ 1 tablespoon of egg beaters

◊ ¼ teaspoon of cinnamon

◊ 2 tablespoons of Walden Farms pancake syrup

Instructions:

◊ To make pancake batter, whisk together all of the ingredients. If you feel that the batter is too thick, add more water.

◊ Pour the batter into a nonstick skillet over a medium-high flame.

◊ Brown one side of the pancake before flipping it over to brown the other.

11.18 Oatmeal Bars

Preparation time: 20 minutes

Servings: 2

Nutrition Facts per Serving: Calories: 194, Carbohydrates: 8g, Sugar: 1.3g, Protein: 6g, Fat: 18g

This recipe is vegetarian-friendly

Ingredients:

◊ 1 tablespoon of egg beaters

◊ 1 oatmeal packet

◊ 3 tablespoons of water

◊ 2 tablespoons of vanilla sugar-free syrup

Instructions:

◊ Preheat the oven to 350 °F.

◊ Combine the ingredients in a mixing bowl. Let it rest for 5 minutes.

◊ Pour the mixture into a ramekin. Bake for 12 minutes. Let cool for 20 minutes then cut the dough into bars, and serve.

11.19 Oatmeal Raisin Cookies

Preparation time: 5 minutes

Servings: 2

Nutrition Facts per Serving: Calories: 156, Carbohydrates: 9g, Sugar: 1g, Protein: 5g, Fat: 4g

This recipe is vegetarian-friendly

Ingredients:

◊ 1/8 teaspoon of cinnamon

◊ 1 packet of oatmeal

◊ 1/8 teaspoon of baking powder

- ◊ 1 packet of oatmeal raisin crunch bar
- ◊ ½ teaspoon of vanilla
- ◊ 1 packet of stevia
- ◊ 2 tablespoons of PB2 – Optional
- ◊ 1/3 cup water

Instructions:

⇒ Preheat the oven to 350 °F.

⇒ Microwave for approximately 15 seconds or until the oatmeal raisin bar is slightly melted.

⇒ Combine all of the ingredients in a mixing bowl and set them aside for 5 minutes.

⇒ Using parchment paper or cooking spray, line a cookie sheet.

⇒ To create 4 cookies, drop by spoonfuls. Preheat oven to 350°F and bake for 12–15 minutes.

11.20 Cinnamon Pancake Buns

Preparation time: 15 minutes

Servings: 2

Nutrition Facts per Serving: Calories: 125, Carbohydrates: 3.5g, Sugar: 1g, Protein: 7g, Fat: 7g

This recipe is vegetarian-friendly

Ingredients:

- ◊ 1 packet of stevia
- ◊ 2 tablespoons of water
- ◊ 1 packet of pancake mix
- ◊ Light cooking spray
- ◊ 1/8 teaspoon of baking powder
- ◊ ¼ teaspoon of vanilla extract
- ◊ ¼ teaspoon of cinnamon

Instructions:

⇒ In a small-sized dish, gently combine all the ingredients.

⇒ Try not to overwork the batter.

⇒ Coat a small microwavable dish or mug with cooking sprau

⇒ Dust the top of the batter with cinnamon and spoon it into the bowl/mug/dish.

⇒ Microwave for 40 seconds in the microwave.

⇒ Wait 2 minutes, then serve.

11.21 Chocolate Cake Stuffed with Peanut Butter or Cream Cheese Icing

Preparation time: 15 minutes

Servings: 2

Nutrition Facts per Serving: Calories: 245, Carbohydrates: g, Sugar: 1g, Protein: 7g, Fat: 23g

This recipe is vegetarian-friendly

Ingredients:

- ◊ 1 packet of brownie mix
- ◊ 2 tablespoons of PB2
- ◊ 1 chocolate chip pancake
- ◊ ¼ cup of plus 2 tablespoons of water
- ◊ 2 tablespoons of Walden Farms chocolate syrup

Instructions:

⇒ To get the required consistency, combine 2 tablespoons of PB2 with approximately 1 tablespoon of water. Remove from the equation.

⇒ Combine ¼ cup + 2 tablespoons of water with the pancake and brownie mixes. ¼ of the batter (or 1 heaping tablespoon) should be divided between two brownie containers or the muffin pans.

⇒ Half of the PB2 or peanut butter should be placed in the middle of each brownie pan. To cover the peanut butter, pour ¼ of the batter into each brownie container.

⇒ Bake for 15 minutes at 350°F or until done. In the microwave for 2 minutes.

⇒ 1 tablespoon of chocolate syrup drizzled over each cake. Enjoy!

11.22 Chocolate Chip Cakes

Preparation time: 25 minutes

Servings: 2

Nutrition Facts per Serving: Calories: 250, Carbohydrates: 9g, Sugar: 1.3g, Protein: 6g, Fat: 22g

This recipe is vegetarian-friendly

Ingredients:

- ◊ 1 packet of brownie or 1 chocolate chip soft bake
- ◊ ¼ teaspoon of baking powder

◊ 1 packet of chocolate chip pancakes

◊ ¼ cup of water

Instructions:

◊ Preheat the oven to 350 °F.

◊ Combine 1 of the pancake packets with the soft bake mix.

◊ Stir in the baking powder and water until everything is well mixed.

◊ Bake for about 20 minutes or until done, dividing the batter between two brownie pans or muffin tins.

11.23 Cinnamon Roll with Cream Cheese Icing

Preparation time: 25 minutes

Servings: 2

Nutrition Facts per Serving: Calories: 155, Carbohydrates: 2.3g, Sugar: 0.5g, Protein: 6g, Fat: 10g

This recipe is vegetarian friendly

Ingredients:

◊ 2 tablespoons of water

◊ 1 packet of stevia, divided

◊ 1 packet of pancake mix

◊ 1/8 teaspoon of cinnamon

◊ Few sprays of I Can't Believe It is Not Butter Spray

◊ 1 tablespoon of light cream cheese

Instructions:

⇒ Combine the pancake mix, 1/2 of the Stevia package, cinnamon, and water in a mixing bowl.

⇒ Fill a small container halfway with the mixture. 50 seconds in the microwave. Be careful not to overcook it, or it will become dry.

⇒ Combine cream cheese and the rest of the stevia in the same bowl that was used to create the pancake batter.

⇒ With the batter that was left in the bowl, play about with it. This incorporates a little amount of the cinnamon mix into the cream cheese mixture.

⇒ Spread the mixture on the pancake and serve.

11.24 Ricotta Vanilla Creme Crepes in Chocolate Sauce

Preparation time: 25 minutes

Servings: 2

Nutrition Facts per Serving: Calories: 100, Carbohydrates: 2g, Sugar: 0.2g, Protein: 6g, Fat: 6g

This recipe is vegetarian friendly

Ingredients:

⇒ ¼ cup of water

⇒ 1/8 teaspoon of vanilla extract

⇒ ¼ cup of part-skim ricotta cheese

⇒ 1 packet of chocolate chip pancake

⇒ ½ packet of Stevia

⇒ 1 tablespoon of Walden Farms chocolate syrup

Instructions:

⇒ Combine the chocolate chip pancake mix and the water in a mixing bowl. It should be a bit thinner than the pancake batter inconsistency. Using cooking spray, coat a nonstick skillet.

⇒ Pour the batter into the pan and heat until the batter is done. Set them aside.

⇒ Blend the Stevia, ricotta cheese, and vanilla essence together until smooth.

⇒ Place the mixture inside the crepe. 1 tablespoon of chocolate syrup drizzled over the top.

11.25 Pancake Muffins

Preparation time: 15 minutes

Servings: 2

Nutrition Facts per Serving: Calories: 211, Carbohydrates: 8g, Sugar: 1g, Protein: 9g, Fat: 18g

This recipe is vegetarian friendly

Ingredients:

◊ 1 packet of pancake mix

◊ ¼ cup of water

Instructions:

◊ In a shaker jar, combine the pancake mix with water. Shake vigorously until fully blended.

◊ Fill a glass mug that has been coated with cooking spray and has the same shape all the way around with the mixture. Alternatively, pour into a tiny square container to use as a bread container.

◊ Microwave for 1 ½ minutes, then remove from glass or container and cut in half.

11.26 Pumpkin Waffles

Preparation time: 20 minutes

Servings: 2

Nutrition Facts per Serving: Calories: 151, Carbohydrates: 6g, Sugar: 1g, Protein: 5g, Fat: 9g

This recipe is vegetarian-friendly

Ingredients:

◊ ¼ teaspoon of pumpkin pie spice

◊ ¼ cup of water

◊ 1 packet of chocolate chip or golden pancake

◊ 1 tablespoon of 100% canned pumpkin

◊ 2 tablespoons of Walden Farms pancake syrup

Instructions:

⇒ Preheat the small dash waffle maker using cooking spray.

⇒ In a small-sized mixing dish, whisk together all of the ingredients, except the pancake syrup.

⇒ Pour half of the batter in the waffle maker.

⇒ Cook until the indicator light goes off or until the food is well cooked.

⇒ Then finish cooking the remaining batter.

⇒ Drizzle with two tablespoons of Walden farm pancake syrup.

11.27 Zucchini Bread

Preparation time: 20 minutes

Servings: 2

Nutrition Facts per Serving: Calories: 166, Carbohydrates: 5g, Sugar: 2g, Protein: 6g, Fat: 15g

This recipe is vegetarian-friendly

Ingredients:

◊ 2 tablespoons of egg beaters

◊ 1 any pancake packet

◊ 1 packet of stevia

◊ ¼ cup of shredded zucchini

◊ 2 tablespoons of water

Instructions:

⇒ Preheat the small dash waffle maker using cooking spray.

⇒ In a small-sized mixing dish, whisk together all of the ingredients, except the pancake syrup.

⇒ Pour half of the batter in the waffle maker.

⇒ Cook until the indicator light goes off or until the food is well cooked.

⇒ Then finish cooking the remaining batter.

⇒ Drizzle with two tablespoons of Walden farm pancake syrup.

11.28 Cream Cheese Filled Chocolate Chip Crepes

Preparation time: 20 minutes

Servings: 2

Nutrition Facts per Serving: Calories: 172, Carbohydrates: 7g, Sugar: 1g, Protein: 6g, Fat: 13g

This recipe is vegetarian-friendly

Ingredients:

◊ ¼ cup of water

◊ 1 tablespoon of Walden Farms fruit spread

◊ 1 packet of chocolate chip pancake

◊ 1 tablespoon of light cream cheese

◊ ½ packet of stevia

Instructions:

⇒ Combine the chocolate chip pancake mix and also the water in a mixing bowl. It should be a bit thinner than pancake batter inconsistency.

⇒ Using cooking spray, coat a nonstick skillet.

⇒ Pour the batter into the pan and heat until the batter is done. Remove from the equation.

⇒ Combine cream cheese and fruit spread (or stevia) in a mixing bowl until well combined.

⇒ Microwave for 15 seconds, stirring after that until well combined. Place the mixture inside the crepe.

11.29 Banana Chocolate Cheesecake Cookies

Preparation time: 20 minutes

Servings: 4

Nutrition Facts per Serving: Calories: 202, Carbohydrates: 19g, Sugar: 9g, Protein: 5g, Fat: 10g

This recipe is vegetarian-friendly

Ingredients:

◊ 4 sachets of brownie

◊ 2 tablespoons of coconut oil

◊ 5 tablespoons of water

◊ 1 banana, mashed

◊ 2 tablespoons of light cream cheese

◊ ¼ teaspoon vanilla

Instructions:

⇒ Preheat the oven to 350°F.

⇒ In a medium-size mixing bowl, crush the brownie, stir in the coconut oil and water.

⇒ Divide the mixture evenly in the bottom of your cupcake liners.

⇒ Press the crumbs down firmly with a teaspoon.

⇒ In another mixing bowl, whisk cream cheese, mashed banana, and vanilla.

⇒ Spoon the batter equally over the prepared crusts and bake for 10 minutes. Let cool for at least 15 minutes and serve.

11.30 Butterscotch Crepes with Caramel Sauce

Preparation time: 20 minutes

Servings: 2

Nutrition Facts per Serving: Calories: 125, Carbohydrates: 2g, Sugar: 0g, Protein: 6g, Fat: 10g

This recipe is vegetarian-friendly

Ingredients:

◊ ¼ cup of water

◊ 1 tablespoon of PB2

◊ 1 packet of pancake mix

◊ 1 packet of vanilla pudding

◊ 1 tablespoon of Walden Farms caramel syrup

◊ ½ cup of water

Instructions:

⇒ Combine ½ cup of water and 1 tablespoon of PB2 in a mixing bowl. Blend everything until it's smooth.

⇒ Refrigerate for 30 minutes before serving.

⇒ Combine the pancake mix and the water in a mixing bowl. It should be a bit thinner than the pancake batter inconsistency.

⇒ Using cooking spray, coat a nonstick skillet.

⇒ Pour the batter into the pan and heat until the batter is done. Remove from the equation.

⇒ Spread 2 to 3 tablespoons of pudding on each crepe and save the remainder for another time. 1 tablespoon of caramel syrup drizzled on top.

11.31 Peanut Butter Ice Cream

Preparation time: 45 minutes

Servings: 2

Nutrition Facts per Serving: Calories: 241, Carbohydrates: 2g, Sugar: 0g, Protein: 5.3g, Fat: 23g

This recipe is vegetarian-friendly

Ingredients:

◊ ½ cup of water

◊ 1 tablespoon of Walden Farms chocolate syrup

◊ 1 packet of chocolate pudding

◊ 1 tablespoon of powdered peanut butter PB2

Instructions:

◊ Whisk together the pudding mix, water, and PB2 in a mixing bowl.

◊ Fill a small container halfway with the mixture. Freeze for about 40 minutes before serving

◊ . Top with Walden Farms Chocolate Syrup before serving. And enjoy!

11.32 Pumpkin Pie Custard

Preparation time: 30 minutes

Servings: 2

Nutrition Facts per Serving: Calories: 235, Carbohydrates: 8g, Sugar: 4g, Protein: 4g, Fat: 19g

This recipe is vegetarian-friendly

Ingredients:

◊ 1 egg white

◊ 1 packet of stevia

◊ 1 package of vanilla pudding

◊ ½ teaspoon of vanilla extract

◊ ½ cup of water

◊ ½ teaspoon of pumpkin pie spice

Instructions:

⇒ Preheat the oven to 350 °F. Coat a ramekin with cooking spray.

⇒ In a blender, combine all of the ingredients. Pour into the ramekin and bake for 20 to 25 minutes, or until set.

⇒ Serve immediately or keep refrigerated overnight.

11.33 Pudding Pies

Preparation time: 20 minutes

Servings: 2

Nutrition Facts per Serving: Calories: 273, Carbohydrates: 7g, Sugar: 1g, Protein: 6g, Fat: 25g

This recipe is vegetarian-friendly

Ingredients:

◊ 1 packet of Splenda

◊ 1 packet of maple and brown sugar oatmeal

◊ ½ teaspoon of baking powder

◊ 1 packet of banana pudding

Instructions:

⇒ Preheat the oven to 350 °F.

⇒ Combine the Splenda, oats, and baking powder in a mixing bowl. Slowly drizzle in the water until the dough barely holds together. Use approximately half a cup of water.

⇒ To make the ramekins, divide the dough into two balls and press into two ramekins that have been coated with cooking spray.

⇒ Bake for 12 minutes. Let it cool for at least 1 hour.

⇒ Mix 4 oz. of water with banana pudding in the shaker jar. Fill each oatmeal cup halfway with the mixture.

⇒ Refrigerate for 30 minutes before serving.

11.34 Fudge Balls

Preparation time: 30 minutes

Servings: 2

Nutrition Facts per Serving: Calories: 81, Carbohydrates: 10g, Sugar: 5g, Protein: 1g, Fat: 4g

This recipe is vegetarian-friendly

Ingredients:

◊ 1 tablespoon of PB2

◊ 1 packet of chocolate shake, divided

◊ 1 tablespoon of Walden Farms caramel

◊ ½ cup of water

◊ 1 packet of chocolate pudding

Instructions:

◊ Set aside 2 tablespoons of a chocolate shake mix. In a small-sized mixing bowl, combine the remaining chocolate shake mix, caramel or chocolate syrup, pudding mix, and PB2.

◊ Slowly drizzle in a little less than a half cup of water until the dough is stiff enough to roll into balls. Form the mixture into balls.

◊ Roll the balls in the shake mix that has been set aside.

◊ Refrigerate for 30 minutes or until hard.

11.35 Brownie Pudding Cups

Preparation time: 20 minutes

Servings: 2

Nutrition Facts per Serving: Calories: 152, Carbohydrates: 6g, Sugar: 1g, Protein: 7g, Fat: 8g

This recipe is vegetarian-friendly

Ingredients:

◊ 1 packet of chocolate pudding mix

◊ 1 packet of brownie mix

◊ 2 tablespoons of Walden Farms caramel syrup

Instructions:

⇒ In a small-sized mixing dish, combine 3 tablespoons of water with brownie mix. Pour the batter into two ramekins. 1 minute in the microwave. Let cool completely before serving.

⇒ In a small dish, combine pudding and ½ cup of water. Combine the pudding mix and brownies in two ramekins. 1 tablespoon caramel syrup drizzled over each brownie pudding cup. With a knife, swirl the caramel into the pudding.

⇒ Refrigerate until ready to use.

11.36 Cheesecake Ice Cream

Preparation time: 30 minutes

Servings: 2

Nutrition Facts per Serving: Calories: 214, Carbohydrates: 2g, Sugar: 1g, Protein: 2g, Fat: 22g

This recipe is vegetarian-friendly

Ingredients:

◊ ½ cup water

◊ ½ teaspoon of lemon extract

◊ Vanilla Pudding

◊ 1 tablespoon of light cream cheese

Instructions:

⇒ In a mixing dish, whisk together all of the ingredients until thoroughly combined.

⇒ Fill a small bowl with the contents and freeze for at least 30 minutes.

⇒ Alternatively, you may reduce the water to ¼ cup and mix in ½ cup ice to immediately make soft serve.

11.37 Pecan Butter Ice Cream

Preparation time: 10 minutes

Servings: 2

Nutrition Facts per Serving: Calories: 290, Carbohydrates: 3g, Sugar: 1g, Protein: 1g, Fat: 22g

This recipe is vegetarian-friendly

Ingredients:

◊ ¼ teaspoon of coconut extract

◊ 1 packet of vanilla pudding

◊ ½ teaspoon of maple extract

◊ ½ cup of crushed ice cubes

◊ ¼ teaspoon of almond extract

◊ ¾ cup of water

◊ 1 tablespoon of Walden Farms caramel syrup

Instructions:

⇒ In a blender, combine all of the ingredients. Combine ingredients in a blender for 2 to 3 minutes, or until smooth.

11.38 Green Tea Smoothie

Preparation time: 10 minutes

Servings: 2

Nutrition Facts per Serving: Calories: 107, Carbohydrates: 7g, Sugar: 1g, Protein: 6g, Fat: 6g

This recipe is vegetarian-friendly

Ingredients:

◊ 1 cup of baby spinach

◊ 1 packet of vanilla shake

◊ 1 cup of cashew or almond milk unsweetened

◊ Few cubes of ice

◊ ½ cup of plain 2% Greek yogurt

◊ ½ teaspoon of Matcha green tea powder

Instructions:

⇒ In a blender, combine all of the Ingredients.

⇒ Put it into a glass and take a sip.

11.39 Pina Colada Shake

Preparation time: 10 minutes

Servings: 2

Nutrition Facts per Serving: Calories: 206, Carbohydrates: 7g, Sugar: 4g, Protein: 1g, Fat: 12g

This recipe is vegetarian-friendly

Ingredients:

◊ ½ cup of diet ginger ale

◊ 1 packet of vanilla shake

◊ 1/8 teaspoon of coconut extract

◊ ¼ cup plus 2 tablespoons of water

◊ 1/8 teaspoon of rum extract

◊   3 to 4 ice cubes

◊   ¼ teaspoon of pineapple extract

Instructions:

◊   Combine all ingredients in a blender and serve.

11.40 Mango Pineapple Pancakes

Preparation time: 20 minutes

Servings: 2

Nutrition Facts per Serving: Calories: 198, Carbohydrates: 5g, Sugar: 2g, Protein: 4g, Fat: 11g

This recipe is vegetarian-friendly

Ingredients:

◊   1 packet of pineapple mango smoothie

◊   1 egg white

◊   2 tablespoons of water

◊   ¼ teaspoon of baking powder

Instructions:

⇒   In a small-sized mixing dish, combine all of the ingredients. Remove from the equation.

⇒   Using cooking spray, coat a small nonstick skillet.

⇒   Heat to a medium-high temperature.

⇒   Pour the pancake batter into a hot skillet.

⇒   After one minute, or when bubbles form in the middle, flip the board.

⇒   Cook for another minute.

⇒   Enjoy!

11.41 Pistachio Shake

Preparation time: 10 minutes

Servings: 2

Nutrition Facts per Serving: Calories: 289, Carbohydrates: 7g, Sugar: 1g, Protein: 7g, Fat: 27g

Per serving: fueling: 1, condiment: 2, green: 1

This recipe is vegetarian-friendly

Ingredients:

◊   1 cup of baby spinach

◊   1 packet of French vanilla shake

◊   ¼ cup of water

◊   1 ½ teaspoons of sugar-free pistachio pudding

◊   ½ cup of unsweetened cashew milk

◊   Ice

Instructions:

⇒   In a blender, combine all ingredients and mix until smooth. Serve.

11.42 Pumpkin Spice Frappuccino

Preparation time: 10 minutes

Servings: 2

Nutrition Facts per Serving: Calories: 167, Carbohydrates: 3g, Sugar: 1g, Protein: 1g, Fat: 18g

This recipe is vegetarian-friendly

Ingredients:

◊   ½ cup of unsweetened cashew milk

◊   ¼ teaspoon of pumpkin spice

◊   3/4 cups of cold coffee

◊   1 tablespoon of pumpkin puree

◊   1 package of packet of French vanilla shake

◊   1 tablespoon of Walden Farms walnut maple syrup

◊   ¼ teaspoon of ground cinnamon

Instructions:

⇒   In a blender, combine all of the ingredients.

⇒   Blend in the appropriate quantity of ice until smooth.

11.43 Root Beer Float

Preparation time: 10 minutes

Servings: 2

Nutrition Facts per Serving: Calories: 205, Carbohydrates: 2g, Sugar: 0.1g, Protein: 1.2g, Fat: 22g

This recipe is vegetarian-friendly

Ingredients:

◊   ½ cup to 1 cup of ice

◊   1 packet of vanilla shake

◊   1 cup of diet root beer

Instructions:

⇒   In a blender, combine all of the ingredients and mix until smooth.

11.44 Shake Cake Muffins

Preparation time: 20 minutes

Servings: 2

Nutrition Facts per Serving: Calories: 285, Carbohydrates: 8g, Sugar: 1g, Protein: 9g, Fat: 24g

This recipe is vegetarian-friendly

Ingredients:

◊ 2 tablespoons of egg beaters or egg whites

◊ 1 shake packet

◊ ¼ teaspoon of baking powder

◊ 2 tablespoons of water

Instructions:

⇒ Preheat the oven to 350 °F.

⇒ After mixing the dry ingredients, add the wet components.

⇒ Fill two muffin tins halfway with batter.

⇒ Bake until done, about 16 to 18 minutes.

⇒ Let cool completely before serving.

11.45 Egg and Cheese Bagel

Preparation time: 15 minutes

Servings: 2

Nutrition Facts per Serving: Calories: 218, Carbohydrates: 3g, Sugar: 1g, Protein: 14g, Fat: 16g

This recipe is vegetarian-friendly

Ingredients:

◊ 1 teaspoon of everything bagel seasoning

◊ 2 sachets of buttermilk cheddar herb biscuit

◊ 2 slices of low-fat cheddar cheese

◊ 3 tablespoons of cold water

◊ 2 eggs

◊ Light cooking spray

Instructions:

⇒ Preheat the oven to 350°F.

⇒ Mix together biscuit sachet with water and distribute evenly among slots of donut pan.

⇒ Sprinkle seasoning on top and bake for 15 minutes or until the edges of the bagel are golden brown.

⇒ In the meantime, cook eggs in an oiled skillet.

⇒ Top each bagel piece with cheese and egg, then top with another half of the bagel piece. Enjoy!

11.46 Cheesecake Chocolate Shake

Preparation time: 10 minutes

Servings: 2

Nutrition Facts per Serving: Calories: 172, Carbohydrates: 4g, Sugar: 1g, Protein: 3g, Fat: 16g

This recipe is vegetarian-friendly

Ingredients:

◊ ¼ cup plus 2 tablespoons of water

◊ 1/8 teaspoon of coconut extract

◊ ½ cup of diet ginger ale

◊ 1 packet of vanilla shake

◊ 3 to 4 ice cubes

◊ ¼ teaspoon of pineapple extract

◊ 1/8 teaspoon of rum extract

Instructions:

⇒ In a blender, combine together the cottage cheese, chocolate shake mix, vanilla extract, cashew or almond milk, and ice.

⇒ Blend until the mixture is completely smooth and serve.

11.47 Mint Chocolate Soft Serve Brownie Bottoms

Preparation time: 15 minutes

Servings: 2

Nutrition Facts per Serving: Calories: 151, Carbohydrates: 4g, Sugar: 1g, Protein: 2g, Fat: 15g

This recipe is vegetarian-friendly

Ingredients:

◊ 1 packet of chocolate mint soft serve

◊ 1 packet of brownie

◊ ½ cup + 3 tablespoons of water, divided

Instructions:

⇒ Using cooking spray, coat two ramekins. Combine the brownie mix and 3 tablespoons of water in a mixing bowl, then divide between two prepared plates. Microwave for 50 seconds, or until well cooked. Let cool completely before serving.

⇒ Combine soft serve and ½ cup of water. Divide the ingredients equally between the two brownies. Freeze for 1 hour before serving.

11.48 Soft Serve Cookies

Preparation time: 20 minutes

Servings: 2

Nutrition Facts per Serving: Calories: 180, Carbohydrates: 5g, Sugar: 1g, Protein: 4g, Fat: 16g

This recipe is vegetarian-friendly

Ingredients:

◊ 2 tablespoons of egg beaters

◊ 1 soft serve

◊ ½ teaspoon of baking powder

◊ 3 tablespoons of water

Instructions:

⇒ Preheat the oven to 350 °F.

⇒ Combine all of the ingredients in a mixing bowl and whisk until well combined.

⇒ Using a spoon, drop cookies one at a time.

⇒ Bake for 12 minutes. Let completely cool before serving.

11.49 Chewy Chocolate Chip Cookies

Preparation time: 25 minutes

Servings: 2

Nutrition Facts per Serving: Calories: 130, Carbohydrates: 5g, Sugar: 1g, Protein: 3g, Fat: 12g

This recipe is vegetarian-friendly

Ingredients:

◊ 4 tablespoons of water

◊ 1 packet of brownie soft bake

◊ 2 tablespoons of powdered peanut butter

◊ Additional water for the powdered peanut butter

◊ 1 chocolate chip soft bake

Instructions:

⇒ Preheat the oven to 375 °F.

⇒ Using parchment paper, line a baking sheet.

⇒ In a small-sized mixing dish, combine all of the ingredients.

⇒ Form two cookies with the batter on parchment paper.

⇒ Because the dough will be sticky, flatten the cookies using moist palms.

⇒ Bake for 14-15 minutes, or until done.

⇒ Mix together 1 to 1 ½ tablespoons of powdered peanut butter + 1 to 1 ½ tablespoons of water. Drizzle the powdered peanut butter mixture on top of the cookies after they've cooled.

11.50 Brownies Stuffed with Peanut Butter and Cream Cheese

Preparation time: 20 minutes

Servings: 2

Nutrition Facts per Serving: Calories: 245, Carbohydrates: 8g, Sugar: 1g, Protein: 6g, Fat: 23g

This recipe is vegetarian-friendly

Ingredients:

◊ 1 tablespoon of PB2

◊ 1 packet of brownie

◊ 1 tablespoon of light cream cheese

Instructions:

⇒ Add 3 tablespoons of water to the brownie mix and whisk until mixed, as instructed on the back of the box. Remove from the equation.

⇒ Microwave cream cheese for about 10 seconds or until softened. Toss the softened cream cheese with PB2 and ½ tablespoon of water. Stir until the mixture is smooth and creamy.

⇒ Pour half of the brownie mixture into the disposable containers that came with the brownies coated with cooking spray.

⇒ Over the brownie mixture, spoon the peanut buttercream mixture and spread evenly.

⇒ Distribute the remaining brownie mixture over the top evenly.

⇒ Microwave for about 1 minute and 30 seconds. Let completely cool before serving.

11.51 Peanut Butter Brownie Greek Yogurt

Preparation time: 20 minutes

Servings: 2

Nutrition Facts per Serving: Calories: 91, Carbohydrates: 15g, Sugar: 1g, Protein: 3g, Fat: 3g

This recipe is vegetarian-friendly

Ingredients:

◊ 2 tablespoons of reduced-fat plain Greek yogurt

◊ 1 tablespoon of PB2

◊ 1 packet of brownie

Instructions:

⇒ In a medium mixing dish, add the three ingredients and whisk until well mixed. It will be a thick mixture.

⇒ Serve and enjoy!

11.52 Silky Brownies

Preparation time: 30 minutes

Servings: 2

Nutrition Facts per Serving: Calories: 102, Carbohydrates: 3g, Sugar: 1g, Protein: 2g, Fat: 9g

This recipe is vegetarian friendly

Ingredients:

◊ 1 packet chocolate chip soft bake

◊ 1 tablespoon of Walden Farms sugar-free caramel syrup

◊ 1 packet of brownie

◊ ¼ cup of 1% cottage cheese

Instructions:

⇒ Make the brownie batter according to the package instructions, then divide it into two tiny ramekins.

⇒ Prepare your soft bake as per the package instructions and put it aside.

⇒ To remove the lumps, mix the cottage cheese with syrup in a small-sized blender. Spread the cottage cheese mixture on the brownie, then sprinkle the soft bake with a few drips.

⇒ Microwave for 1 minute. Warm-up or freeze for 30 minutes before eating.

11.53 Pizza Bread or Tomato Bread

Preparation time: 20 minutes

Servings: 2

Nutrition Facts per Serving: Calories: 117, Carbohydrates: 4g, Sugar: 1g, Protein: 7g, Fat: 8g

This recipe is vegetarian-friendly

Ingredients:

◊ ¼ teaspoon of baking powder

◊ 1 cream of tomato soup

◊ 2 tablespoons water

Instructions:

⇒ Preheat the oven to 425 °F.

⇒ Use parchment paper or spray a baking sheet with cooking spray.

⇒ Combine the soup, seasonings, baking powder, and water in a mixing bowl. Form a circle with the batter on the prepared cookie sheet.

⇒ Cook for 5 minutes before flipping with a spatula. If you want to add the cheese after flipping, do so now. Return the bread to the oven for another 5 minutes.

⇒ Once the bread is done baking, sprinkle the laughing cow cheese on top and serve.

11.54 Grilled Tomato Cheese Sandwich

Preparation time: 20 minutes

Servings: 2

Nutrition Facts per Serving: Calories: 315, Carbohydrates: 4.7g, Sugar: 1g, Protein: 11g, Fat: 29g

This recipe is vegetarian-friendly

Ingredients:

◊ ¼ cup of egg beaters

◊ 1 packet of cream of tomato soup

◊ 1 slice of 2% low-fat American cheese

Instructions:

⇒ Combine the soup and the egg beaters in a mixing bowl.

⇒ Fill a sandwich maker with the mixture and distribute it equally among the four squares. Cook for 3 to 4 minutes.

⇒ Fold in ½ and fill with cheese in the center. Enjoy!

11.55 Faux Fried Zucchini

Preparation time: 30 minutes

Servings: 2

Nutrition Facts per Serving: Calories: 213, Carbohydrates: 4g, Sugar: 2g, Protein: 21g, Fat: 15g

This recipe is vegetarian-friendly

Ingredients:

◊   1 ½ cups of thinly sliced zucchini

◊   ¼ teaspoon of black pepper

◊   Light cooking spray

◊   1 packet cream of broccoli soup

◊   2 teaspoons of olive oil

◊   ¼ teaspoon of garlic powder

Instructions:

⇒ Preheat the oven to 400 °F.

⇒ Using olive oil, coat zucchini slices.

⇒ Combine the soup and seasonings in a gallon Ziploc bag.

⇒ Toss in the zucchini slices and toss to coat.

⇒ Refrigerate for 10 minutes after marinating.

⇒ Apply nonstick cooking spray to a cookie sheet and arrange zucchini in a single layer.

⇒ Bake for 12 minutes, or until the edges are golden brown.

⇒ Broil for 3 minutes on the other side, or until uniformly browned.

11.56 Grasshopper Parfaits

Preparation time: 10 minutes

Servings: 2

Nutrition Facts per Serving: Calories: 261, Carbohydrates: 5g, Sugar: 1g, Protein: 3g, Fat: 25g

This recipe is vegetarian-friendly

Ingredients:

◊   3/4 cup of plain non-fat Greek yogurt

◊   1 sachet of double chocolate brownie

◊   ¼ cup of whipped topping

◊   ¼ cup of unsweetened almond milk

◊   3 pinch of green food coloring

◊   1 sachet of creamy vanilla shake

◊   1/8 teaspoon of peppermint extract

Instructions:

⇒ Follow the package instructions to make a delicious double chocolate brownie. Let completely cool before crumbling.

⇒ Mix creamy vanilla shake, peppermint essence, Greek yogurt, milk, and green food coloring until blended in a medium-sized mixing basin.

⇒ Fill two pint-sized mason jars halfway with brownie crumbs. Place a quarter of the yogurt mixture on top of each. Once again, repeat the layers.

⇒ Serve with a dollop of whipped cream.

11.57 Greek Yogurt Cookie Dough

Preparation time: 5 minutes

Servings: 2

Nutrition Facts per Serving: Calories: 160, Carbohydrates: 3g, Sugar: 1.3g, Protein: 8g, Fat: 7g

This recipe is vegetarian-friendly

Ingredients:

◊   ½ cup of low-fat Greek yogurt

◊   1 sachet of chewy chocolate chip cookie

Instructions:

⇒ Chill until ready to serve by mixing the Chewy Chocolate Chip Cookie sachet with Greek yogurt.

11.58 Lemon Meringue Bites

Preparation time: 5 minutes

Servings: 6

Nutrition Facts per Serving: Calories: 181, Carbohydrates: 1.2g, Sugar: 0g, Protein: 3g, Fat: 1.5g

This recipe is vegetarian-friendly

Ingredients:

◊   1 ½ cups of low-fat Greek yogurt

◊   ½ teaspoon of lime zest

◊   2 sachets of zesty lemon crisp bars

◊   1 teaspoon of sugar-free lemon gelatin

Instructions:

⇒   Line 6 cupcake liners in a muffin pan. Every Zesty Lemon Crisp

⇒   Bar should be cut into thirds. Microwave on high for 10-15 seconds. To make a thin crust, press every bar piece into the Six cupcake liners.

⇒   Combine the yogurt and gelatin powder in a microwave-safe bowl.

⇒   Microwave for 1 minute on high; stir after 1 minute, then cook for another minute. Top each of the 6 crusts with ¼ cup of the yogurt mixture.

⇒   Let chill for at least 1 hour. Serve with lime zest as a garnish. (optional)

11.59 Chocolate Pumpkin Cheesecake

Preparation time: 50 minutes

Servings: 2

Nutrition Facts per Serving: Calories: 283, Carbohydrates: 6g, Sugar: 1g, Protein: 5g, Fat: 23g

This recipe is vegetarian-friendly

Ingredients:

◊   2 tablespoons of cold water

◊   3 tablespoons of pumpkin puree

◊   2 sachets of double chocolate brownie

◊   ½ teaspoon of pumpkin pie spice

◊   ½ tablespoon of unsalted butter melted

◊   Light cooking spray

◊   2 packets of Stevia

◊   1 pinch of salt

◊   1 cup of plain non-fat Greek Yogurt

◊   1 large egg

◊   ½ teaspoon of vanilla extract

Instructions:

⇒   Preheat the oven to 350°F.

⇒   Combine the butter, Decadent Double Chocolate Brownies, and water in a small-sized mixing dish.

⇒   Divide the brownie batter equally between the two small spring form pans that have been gently oiled. To make thin crusts, press brownies mixture into the bottoms of the pans. 15 minutes in the oven

⇒   In a medium-sized mixing bowl, add the other ingredients while the brownies are baking. Blend until completely smooth. Divide the batter equally between the two spring form pans.

⇒   Reduce the temperature of the oven at 300°F. Bake for 35 to 40 minutes, or until the sides are brown and the middle is nearly set.

⇒   Remove the rims once they have cooled.

11.60 Grilled Smash Potato Cheese

Preparation time: 15 minutes

Servings: 2

Nutrition Facts per Serving: Calories: 193, Carbohydrates: 8g, Sugar: 3g, Protein: 3g, Fat: 6g

This recipe is vegetarian-friendly

Ingredients:

◊   1 cup of water

◊   2 sachets of smashed potatoes

◊   1 cup of low-fat cheddar cheese shredded

Instructions:

⇒   Preheat the waffle iron.

⇒   Mix smashed potatoes and water in a medium microwave-safe bowl until fully mixed. Microwave for 1 ½ minutes on high, then stir.

⇒   Spray a heated waffle iron lightly with cooking spray before pouring the batter into it. Close the cover and cook for 10 to 12 minutes, or until done.

⇒   Open the cover and spread half of the waffle with cheese of your choice (mozzarella, low-fat shredded Cheddar, or Pepper Jack) (two of the four).

⇒   Fold the second half of the waffle over, cover the waffle iron top, and cook for another 1 to 2 minutes, or until the cheese has melted.

11.61 Caprese Pizza Bites

Preparation time: 20 minutes

Servings: 2

Nutrition Facts per Serving: Calories: 135, Carbohydrates: 4g, Sugar: 3g, Protein: 9g, Fat: 9g

This recipe is vegetarian-friendly

Ingredients:

◊ 2 teaspoons of olive oil

◊ 2 tablespoons of fresh mozzarella log chopped

◊ 4 sachets of buttermilk cheddar herb biscuit

◊ 3 small, sliced Roma tomatoes

◊ ½ cup of unsweetened Almond Milk

◊ Light cooking spray

◊ 2 tablespoons of balsamic vinegar

◊ 1 cup of basil leaves

Instructions:

⇒ Preheat the oven to 450 °F.

⇒ Combine the milk (unsweetened almond or cashew milk), buttermilk cheddar herb biscuit, and oil in a medium-sized mixing dish.

⇒ In a norm, lightly-greased muffin pan, divide biscuit mixture equally among the holes.

⇒ Each muffin pan slot should be layered with a slice of mozzarella, a slice of tomato, and a few basil leaves.

⇒ Bake for 12 minutes, or until the biscuit mixture is golden brown and the cheese has melted.

⇒ Before serving, drizzle with balsamic vinegar.

11.62 Green Smoothie with Coconut and Hemp

Preparation time: 10 minutes

Servings: 2

Nutrition Facts per Serving: Calories: 263, Carbohydrates: 10g, Sugar: 0.1g, Protein: 6g, Fat: 24g

This recipe is vegetarian-friendly

Ingredients:

◊ ½ cup of cucumber, sliced

◊ 1 tablespoon of fresh mint

◊ 1 cup of raw baby spinach

◊ ½ cup of refrigerated unsweetened coconut milk

◊ 1 sachet of green renewal shake

◊ 1 celery stalk, chopped

◊ 1 small Ice

◊ 1 stalk of kale

◊ 1 tablespoon of Hemp Seeds

Instructions:

◊ In a blender, combine all ingredients and mix on high for 1 to 2 minutes until desired consistency is achieved.

11.63 Spinach Cheesy Smashed Potatoes

Preparation time: 10 minutes

Servings: 2

Nutrition Facts per Serving: Calories: 247, Carbohydrates: 6g, Sugar: 2g, Protein: 7g, Fat: 22g

This recipe is vegetarian-friendly

Ingredients:

◊ 1 cup of baby spinach

◊ 1 sachet of roasted garlic creamy smashed Potatoes

◊ ½ cup of low-fat shredded mozzarella cheese

◊ 1 teaspoon of water

◊ 1 teaspoon of grated Parmesan

Instructions:

⇒ Follow the package instructions for making roasted garlic creamy smashed Potatoes.

⇒ Microwave the spinach for one minute, or until wilted, with a little water.

⇒ Combine the mozzarella, spinach, and Parmesan cheese with the roasted garlic creamy smashed Potatoes.

11.64 Caramel Crunch Parfait

Preparation time: 10 minutes

Servings: 2

Nutrition Facts per Serving: Calories: 161, Carbohydrates: 4.3g, Sugar: 1g, Protein: 5g, Fat: 15g

This recipe is vegetarian-friendly

Ingredients:

◊ ¼ teaspoon of vanilla Extract

◊ 2 tablespoons of light pressurized whipped topping

◊ 1 sachet of puffed sweet and salty Snacks

◊ 1 tablespoon of sugar-free caramel syrup

◊ 4 tablespoons of low-fat Greek yogurt

◊ 2 tablespoons of light pressurized Whipped Topping

Instructions:

⇒ In a jar or small-sized dish, combine vanilla essence, yogurt, and Stevia.

⇒ Puffed sweet and salty snacks should be crushed into tiny bits (optional).

⇒ Whipped topping and crumbled puffed crackers go on top of the yogurt. Drizzle the syrup over the top.

11.65 Biscuit Pizza

Preparation time: 15 minutes

Servings: 2

Nutrition Facts per Serving: Calories: 109, Carbohydrates: 2g, Sugar: 0.1g, Protein: 6g, Fat: 9g

This recipe is vegetarian-friendly

Ingredients:

◊ Light cooking spray

◊ 1 sachet of buttermilk cheddar herb biscuit

◊ ¼ cup of low-fat cheese

◊ 2 tablespoons of cold water

◊ 2 tablespoons of Rao's homemade sauce

Instructions:

⇒ Preheat the oven to 350 °F.

⇒ Combine the biscuit mix with water in a tiny, thin, crust shape on a foil-lined baking sheet that has been lightly coated with cooking spray. Bake for about 10 minutes in the oven

⇒ After baking for 10 minutes, cover with tomato sauce (like Rao's Homemade) and mozzarella, and bake for another 4-5 minutes, or until the cheese is melted.

11.66 French Toast Sticks

Preparation time: 20 minutes

Servings: 2

Nutrition Facts per Serving: Calories: 142, Carbohydrates: 1g, Sugar: 0.1g, Protein: 8g, Fat: 11g

This recipe is vegetarian-friendly

Ingredients:

◊ 2 tablespoons of low-fat cream cheese

◊ Light cooking spray

◊ 2 sachets of cinnamon crunchy O's cereal

◊ 2 tablespoons of sugar-free syrup

◊ 6 tablespoons of liquid egg substitute

Instructions:

⇒ Grind the Cinnamon Crunchy O's Cereal into a fine breadcrumb-like texture in a food processor or blender.

⇒ Pour the processed Cinnamon Crunchy O's into a big mixing dish, mix liquid egg-substitute and (softened) cream cheese, and stir until a dough forms. Make Six French toast stick portions out of the dough.

⇒ Lightly cook the french toast sticks in a pan sprayed with cooking spray and heated over medium-high flame until warm and nicely browned on both sides.

⇒ Serve with a side of syrup. (Optional)

11.67 Coconut Colada

Preparation time: 10 minutes

Servings: 2

Nutrition Facts per Serving: Calories: 166, Carbohydrates: 1.2g, Sugar: 0.7g, Protein: 1g, Fat: 8g

This recipe is vegetarian-friendly

Ingredients:

◊ ¼ cup of unsweetened coconut milk

◊ ¼ teaspoon of rum extract

◊ ¾ cup of diet ginger ale

◊ 1 sachet of creamy vanilla shake

◊ 2 tablespoons of unsweetened coconut milk, divided

◊   ½ cup of ice

Instructions:

⇒ Combine the Creamy Vanilla Shake, diet ginger ale, coconut milk, rum essence, 2 tablespoons of unsweetened shredded coconut, and Ice in a blender. Blend until smooth and frosty in a blender.

⇒ Fill 2 Pina colada glasses halfway with the mixture and top with the other 2 tablespoons of shredded coconut. Serve right away.

11.68 Skinny Peppermint Mocha

Preparation time: 5 minutes

Servings: 2

Nutrition Facts per Serving: Calories: 39, Carbohydrates: 2g, Sugar: 0.5g, Protein: 1g, Fat: 3g

This recipe is vegetarian-friendly

Ingredients:

◊   1 cup of freshly brewed coffee

◊   1/8 teaspoon of peppermint extract

◊   2 tablespoons of pressurized whipped topping

◊   1 sachet of Velvety Hot Chocolate

◊   ¼ cup of unsweetened vanilla almond milk

◊   1 pinch of cinnamon (optional)

Instructions:

⇒ Mix together 1 sachet of Velvety Hot Chocolate, freshly made coffee of your choice, and ¼ cup reheated unsweetened vanilla almond/cashew milk.

⇒ Spoon into a coffee cup or mug. Stir in the Velvety Hot Chocolate until it has fully dissolved.

⇒ Finish with a dollop of whipped cream and a sprinkling of cinnamon. Enjoy!

11.69 Avacado Toast

Preparation time: 15 minutes

Servings: 2

Nutrition Facts per Serving: Calories: 234, Carbohydrates: 9g, Sugar: 1g, Protein: 7g, Fat: 18g

This recipe is vegetarian-friendly

Ingredients:

◊   ½ cup avocado mashed

◊   1 sachet of buttermilk cheddar herb biscuit

Instructions:

⇒ Follow the package instructions for baking the Biscuit Cheddar Herb Biscuit. Bake in a lightly oiled ramekin for optimum results."

⇒ Let it cool before adding the mashed avocado on top.

11.70 Greek Yogurt Breakfast Bark

Preparation time: 15 minutes

Servings: 2

Nutrition Facts per Serving: Calories: 29, Carbohydrates: 5g, Sugar: 4g, Protein: 2g, Fat: 1g

This recipe is vegetarian-friendly

Ingredients:

◊   1 to 2 packets of low-calorie sugar substitute

◊   1 cup of plain non-fat Greek yogurt

◊   1 sachet of red berry crunchy O's cereal

Instructions:

⇒ Combine Greek yogurt and sugar substitute in a medium-sized mixing dish.

⇒ Line an 8" x 8" baking dish with nonstick foil. In the base of the baking dish, spread Greek yogurt in an equal layer.

⇒ On top of the yogurt, add the Red Berry Crunchy O's Cereal.

⇒ Freeze for 4-5 hours or overnight until the bark is firm.

⇒ Using a sharp knife, cut the bark into smaller pieces. Keep leftovers in the freezer in freezer-safe bags or containers.

Conclusion

The Lean and Green diet will help you lose weight and transform your body very quickly. You can use the information in this book to choose the right program for you, set your goal, and let the delicious recipes help you enjoy the journey.

After the starting phase, it will be easy for you to choose the next food plan to maintain your amazing results in the long run.

I have created this collection of recipes specifically for food enthusiasts, so you don't have to lose your taste buds. As you try these yummy recipes, you can enjoy your diet plan as if you were eating normally with this wide range of mouthwatering options.

This handy guide mixes flavors and smells from Asia, Africa, the Middle East, Europe, and America. Nutritional values are also included to check your dietary needs.

You can use this guide answer all your questions about the Lean and Green diet in one place.

My DIY Fueling recipes will help you sticking to this diet when you run out of packaged Fuelings and save a lot of money too!

Mixing and matching the recipes in this book allows you to vary your diet and get more than 1,500 days of delicious Lean and Green meals. You won't even feel like you're on a diet and will achieve your goals effortlessly.

I thank you for purchasing this book and appreciate it.

I hope you will keep it with you and that you follow it at all times during the exciting journey to your complete body transformation and your switch to your healthy, joyful lifestyle.

If you enjoyed this book, please scan the code and leave a honest review on Amazon.

Thank you so much!

SCAN ME

Made in the USA
Las Vegas, NV
28 December 2023

83630882R00057